Dedication To our three beautiful and amazing children, Skylar, Mia and Sunny, with love....

Acknowledgements I would like to thank the following people for the creation of this, my second book.
Firstly, thank you to my wonderful husband Rob and three wonderful children. Thank you Rob for your constant support, time and encouragement, as well as helping me juggle my time between writing and my family. My children Skylar and Mia were my real inspirations and guinea pigs, without them I would never have written this book. It was through having them and bringing up my own family which opened my eyes to this whole new world, also thanks for eating my food and testing it all for me. I am truly thankful to my mum who taught me not only how to cook but to enjoy and take great pleasure in cooking and therefore instilling me with a passion for food with all her delicious meals. Not only to her but to both my mum and papa for my healthy, fun and natural upbringing which helped shape the way I rear my own family and my attitudes towards healthy eating. I would like to say a huge thanks to Sophia Milligan for her time and perfect photographs which helped show my recipes in the delicious way I had hoped. I would like to say a big thank you to Anne Dolamore of Grub Street for taking the time to talk to me, look at my work and offer invaluable advice and encouragement, and for believing in me and therefore publishing my book.

A big thank you to Tommee Tippee for their fantastic tableware and in particular their PR manager Avril Deane for her positive encouragement and support from the very beginning.

Published in 2007 by
Grub Street, 4 Rainham Close, London SW11 6SS
Email: food@grubstreet.co.uk Web: www.grubstreet.co.uk

Text copyright © Caitilin Finch 2007
Copyright this edition © Grub Street 2007
Designed by Lizzie Ballantyne
Photographs by Sophia Milligan

A CIP block for this book is available from the British Library

ISBN 978-1-904943-91-4

Printed and bound in Slovenia

Disclaimer The information contained in these pages has been written only from my experiences as a mother, not as a nutritionist and is not intended to replace any professional medical advice and should not be used as a basis for diagnosis or choice of treatment. Reactions to different foods will be different for everyone and answers to specific food allergies may not apply to everyone. If you're worried, see your GP immediately.

Contents

  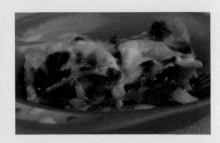

Introduction

As a full-time mother of three children, a newborn, a 3 and a 5 year old, I can fully understand the many uncertainties and questions asked by parents every day when it comes to bringing up a family. I was raised by self-sufficient parents on a farm by the sea near Land's End, Cornwall. I am the eldest of four siblings. We were brought up on a varied, nutritious and healthy diet and from a very young age I always loved helping my parents not only with the cooking (and eating), but also the growing and harvesting of the fruit, vegetables, milk, eggs, honey and grains.

A nutritious diet is vital for everyone, in particular growing children and it does not have to be difficult, time consuming or expensive. A healthy lifestyle begins at home where a child's strongest role models will be and where a lot of their habits will begin – in particular with regards to eating.

After 12 months of age, there are few foods a child cannot have; they should be offered a variety of different foods, flavours and textures. Children will learn to eat what the family eats if they are given the same food and encouraged to try it. As a mother of two toddlers I completely understand the issues arising around mealtimes. However I very quickly realised that the less fuss that was made the more fun it became – and less stressful. It may seem as though your baby is now 'grown up', however they are still learning many new things every day. Picky eating is very common in toddlers. The world has become an exciting place and food may seem less important to them when there are so many other things to do. This refusing of food put in front of them is a way of showing independence and they just want to see what will happen; it is all part of normal development. Rejecting something does not always mean your child doesn't like it. So try and offer it another day, they may eat it.

Encourage food to be fun, interesting and exciting. Mealtimes should be relaxed and happy so make them a positive experience. In their world food is not just something to eat and they are far from understanding the concept that we have to eat to live, to them it is another new taste, texture and smell, so encourage them and let them enjoy the experience. More importantly share it with them. Let your child explore food by touching it and feeding themselves, and expect some mess, this doesn't matter, it can all easily be cleared away afterwards. Give help if needed, offer them encouragement, but don't ask your child to eat quicker, argue or force your child to eat, it will only put them off and create an issue every time you sit down for a meal. If they want to feed themselves that's great,

give them a spoon and yes, most of the food will end up anywhere but their mouth, but it doesn't matter just pick up a spoon yourself and take turns.

I also feel that it is really important that your toddler sits at the table with you and eats with the family, this way it becomes a fun social experience where they can watch, copy and learn from others. Young children should always be supervised when eating. Encourage your child always to eat sitting down, preventing choking and other accidents.

The food children eat in the first few years is of vital importance, as this is the crucial time when the foundations for future good health are laid. Food and nutrients are the building blocks which help to form strong teeth and bones, muscles and healthy tissues. A good diet can also help to protect against illness. As well as the immediate benefits of a healthy diet there are the long term effects as well; if your child develops healthy eating habits early on they should continue to eat this way but here I can't make promises.

A child's diet also needs special care and planning – the requirements for energy and nutrients are high, but appetites are small and eating habits are likely to be finicky. This means toddlers often have small appetites and need less food. The amount eaten from day-to-day can change dramatically. Although this will naturally worry parents it is entirely normal –

remember that children eat when they're hungry and don't starve themselves so let your child decide whether they will eat and how much they will eat. Their diet needs to be made up of small, frequent, nutrient-dense meals. Healthy snacks are also important to help provide the energy and nutrition your child needs during the day. Focus on lots of different vegetables and fruit, and not the amounts.

A variety of fruit and vegetables can be an enjoyable part of your child's life and most babies eat puréed fruit and vegetables as one of their first solid foods. After the first year however, you may notice your child becomes fussier as they become more independent eaters. If children start to eat less fruit and vegetables from time to time, this may worry parents, but usually it causes no harm. It is not possible to force children to eat more fruit and vegetables but you can encourage them by getting them involved in the shopping for ingredients – get them to help count and choose the fruit and vegetables they like and make it fun, they will really enjoy the experience and then hopefully eat it later on. The best way is to set a good example for them. If you eat and enjoy fruit and vegetables every day, your children may eventually follow your lead. It may take time, but this is how children learn best. So keep trying.

Caitilin Finch

Fussy?

Remember, not all toddlers are fussy, but they will all go through a stage of saying 'no' or 'I don't like' at some point, this is entirely normal and here are a few tips I would give to parents, learnt through my experiences as a mum when feeding toddlers:

Children look up to you as a role model, so by sitting with the family, watching you eat a healthy, balanced and varied diet and being given what you eat will encourage them to try things and eat well too.

Don't worry too much – a toddler's appetite and food intake can vary daily, let them tell you when they're full, and don't force a child to finish all the food on their plate. It only makes the situation more stressful.

Offer small servings and give them more if they are still hungry. It can be very off-putting to have a huge amount of food put in front of you.

Be patient and persevere, keep offering new foods, even if they are rejected at first. This does not necessarily mean they don't like something; it may just take some time to get used to it. Just offer encouragement.

Make mealtimes a positive experience. They should be relaxed and happy, so don't worry if your child makes a mess – everything can be cleared away afterwards. If they are allowed to touch and explore their food they will enjoy the experience more and therefore enjoy eating it.

Involve your child in food preparation and planning, there are a number of fun and healthy recipes later in the book which are perfect for getting your little one involved.

How Much 'Should' They Eat?

Toddlers can eat the same food as adults, but before they're two years old children can't eat large amounts of food at one sitting; they need a lot less than you think. So, until then, just ensure you give your child meals and snacks packed with calories and nutrients. Do remember that children have small stomachs and use a lot of energy – they therefore need to eat little and often to keep them going in their busy fun-filled lives. If your child is active, healthy, and growing and developing normally, then it is likely they are getting plenty to eat.

There is no real food pyramid for toddlers as the Kids' Food Pyramid is for children aged 2-6 years. You can however still use it as a rough guide and remember they only need about quarter the size of an adult serving.

Daily intake:
- 4-5 servings of grains
- 2-3 servings of vegetables
- 1-3 servings of fruits
- 2-3 servings from the milk/dairy group
- 2 servings from the meat and protein group
- a limited amount of fats and sweets.

Major Vitamins and Nutrients and their Food Sources

Iron
For Formation of red blood cells, which carry oxygen around the body. **Source:** Eggs, bread, dried fruit, green leafy vegetables, green beans, meat

Calcium
For Bone and teeth development, blood clotting and nervous system. **Source:** Dairy products, nuts and seeds, dark green vegetables, pulses

Vitamin A
For Essential for healthy skin and cell development. **Source:** Yellow and orange fruit and vegetables, liver, dairy products, dark green vegetables

Vitamin C
For Growth, immune system, absorption of iron (especially non-meat sources). **Source:** Vegetables, potatoes, citrus fruits, berries

Vitamin D
For Good for heart and nervous system. Helps with the formation of healthy bones. **Source:** Dairy products and oily fish

Inside your Healthy Kitchen Cupboard

Here are some suggestions for the essentials of a nutritious food cupboard. The following food types will play a crucial part in any healthy baby, child or adult diet.

Organic or Not?

Everyone always asks me if it is a good idea to buy organic produce. The question is, is organic the healthy choice? I would personally say yes not just because of what it does contain but also what it doesn't contain. On average organic food contains more vitamins and minerals than non-organic. This is due to the fact that the plants are grown in a naturally nutrient-rich soil, without the aid of chemical fertilizers and pesticides. Organic meat comes from trusted sources, from animals reared properly, fed well and treated humanely. Organic meat and milk have been shown to have higher levels of essential fatty acids – necessary for a healthy diet. This is because organic animals eat a natural grass-based diet, whereas non-organic animals will eat a lot of processed feeds to help them put on weight. As well as the foods they eat non-organic animals are given a huge number of antibiotics which in turn will be present in their meat and milk, which is consumed by us and fed to our growing children.

It was having my children that really made me think about organics and in particular organic milk – the thought of feeding my children animal antibiotics really put me off and I will now only buy organic, unless it's not available. Organic milk not only tastes good but has also been found to be higher in important nutrients, in particular vitamins A and E, omega 3 essential fatty acids and antioxidants.

Babies and small children have immature digestive systems and need the very purest and safest foods. So giving your family organic food is the best way to avoid the possible risks of pesticides and additives. For these reasons I would therefore always advise people to buy organic and local produce if they can get hold of it and afford it.

If you cannot afford it, as it is often more expensive than non-organic produce, just ensure that you always thoroughly wash your fruit and vegetables to remove any traces of chemicals and pesticides before using them.

Cereals and Grains

Cereals, also known as 'staple foods' are an important source of energy, carbohydrate, protein and fibre. As well as these properties they include essential vitamins such as vitamin E, some of the B vitamins, sodium, magnesium and zinc. They are generally very cheap to buy and versatile to use. Examples of very common and nutritious cereals /grains include:

Rice is the staple food of half the world's population. It is a quick and easy food to cook containing numerous valuable vitamins, minerals and proteins. It also hosts starches and complex carbohydrates. As one of the most easily digested foods it is a very good first food for your toddler.

Couscous is a tiny soft pale yellow grain made from durum wheat flour or barley. It is so versatile and can be served with combinations of meat, fish, poultry and vegetables with spices and herbs, as well as dried fruit and nuts. I find it a brilliant base for a number of meals as it is so simple to prepare, and it can also be added to soups.

Bulgur, also known as cracked wheat, is a natural food with no chemicals or additives used in its processing. It is high in fibre and a great carbohydrate source. Bulgur goes really well with a number of vegetables and is tasty either hot or cold in a salad.

Buckwheat, although it looks like a grain, is in fact a fruit – however what really counts is its high nutritional value; it is full of protein and B vitamins and is rich in phosphorus, potassium, iron, and calcium. Buckwheat is also great for people with wheat allergies and gluten intolerance.

Oats when rolled are commonly used for porridge and oatcakes, and oat flour is used for baby foods and for ready-to-eat breakfast cereals. It's easy to add a fruity purée to these cereals in place of or with milk, not only adding vitamins, but making a nice change. I also find oats great for adding to yoghurts and smoothies (see page 85).

Pasta

Pasta is a starchy complex carbohydrate. It is readily available in numerous shapes, sizes, colours and flavours. Cook your pasta in plenty of boiling water, salt is not necessary. Pasta was always and still is a favourite with my children and forms a large proportion of my children's diet. It is easy to prepare a number of different nutritious sauces to stir in, perhaps sprinkled with a small amount of grated Cheddar cheese or fresh Parmesan cheese for that added extra protein and calcium.

Beans and Pulses

There is a huge variety of pulses, forming over half the world's protein. Beans and pulses are cheap, very tasty and so easy to store. They are extremely nutritious, low in fats and high in dietary fibre and proteins. However, they lack one of the essential amino acids, but this one is found in grains, and therefore when eaten together they form a complete protein. So if a meal contains pulses try to also include a starch so the protein circle is complete. For example; beans with rice or lentils with couscous.

Lentils are high in fibre and are an excellent source of protein, and B vitamins, especially B3, which is essential for a healthy nervous and digestive systems. High in iron, zinc and calcium, they are a good replacement for red meat. They come in a range of sizes and colours, and having a slightly nutty flavour they are a perfect base for stews and soups, combining very well with a huge number of vegetables. Chickpeas, with their nutty taste, are ideal for casseroles and dips (for example hummus) and contain vitamin B, potassium and iron.

If you are using dried pulses they will need soaking, preferably overnight, and then cooking in the soaking water. They should be boiled quickly for the first 10 minutes and then simmered; this will destroy any potential toxins. They should also be cooked until completely soft to ease digestion.

Don't worry if you haven't time to soak and cook beans: tinned beans are just as nutritious as dried beans, and more convenient. If you use tinned beans, just be sure to rinse them well before you use them.

Vegetables

Vegetables are a natural source of all kinds of nutrients and should form a huge part of one's diet. As there is so much choice today meals can easily be made interesting, colourful and very tasty. In all they provide an abundance of vitamins, iron and folic acid, as well as an important base for starch and complex carbohydrates in a meal.

Dark green leafy vegetables are excellent sources of iron, folic acid and A, B and C group vitamins.

Yellow and orange vegetables such as carrots and peppers are also high in vitamin A.

Even if your child dislikes most vegetables then try carrots as they contain a huge range of vitamins and are often said to be the 'most important vegetable'. No other vegetable or fruit contains as much carotene which the body converts to vitamin A. It is also an excellent source of vitamins B and C. Children often like them because of their sweet flavour and they are great with dips and in soups or finely grated in pasta sauces.

Tomatoes are perfect for mixing with

other vegetables and pulses or to be used as a base for a sauce. When blended down they then have an appealing colour and also provide a host of good vitamins including a large amount of vitamin A as well as vitamins C and E and minerals such as calcium, potassium and iron.

Salad ingredients are really good raw and are therefore easy finger foods or eaten with dips such as hummus or yoghurt.

Corn on the cob is fun for children as they can pick it up with their fingers and eat it. They love its sweet creamy texture and interesting shape. It is one of the few vegetables that is a good source of starchy carbohydrates and is packed with dietary fibre and vitamin C. There are a number of ways to cook this and enjoy it as part of a meal. You can either boil it in a large saucepan of water for about 10 minutes or BBQ it, to do this simply remove the green outer husks (some come from the supermarket with the husks already removed) and put on the BBQ. Turn frequently until slightly browned. Serve with a little butter melted over it.

Potatoes, like rice and pasta are starchy foods that should form at least half of the calorie intake of any good diet. For natural sweetness sweet potatoes make a change and their deep orange colour means they contain more nutrients than an ordinary potato. They are an excellent source of vitamin A (in the form of beta-carotene), a very good source of vitamin C, dietary fibre, vitamin B6, potassium and iron.

Fruit

Fruit is an amazing source of fibre and nutrients and occasionally even more so in its dried form, for example; figs, raisins or apricots. Children should be encouraged to eat a lot of fruit and drink pure fruit juices.

There is a huge range of fresh fruits readily available all year round, and the choices to give your little ones are enormous. Fruits are a vital (and easy) component to all healthy diets and children of all ages love them. Bananas (often a favourite, with even the smallest of babies, due to their sweetness and soft texture) not only hold vital minerals and vitamins such as potassium, they also supply plenty of energy, and one kiwi fruit has more vitamin

C than an orange. Grapes are a favourite with so many children, they have a high antioxidant content beneficial to health and when dried, i.e. raisins, they are a particularly rich source of potassium and iron. Blueberries, raspberries, blackberries and strawberries are brilliant, bright and colourful; perfect sized fruits for little fingers, they are packed full of vitamin C, fibre, folic acid and antioxidants.

There are numerous recipes based around fruits, from a simple fruity kebab, dried fruit bar or fruit smoothie, all of which are a tasty, healthy treat or snack. Since my children were eating finger foods at about 6 months old I have always found myself with some sort of fruit (dried or fresh) ready to hand when they say those words 'I'm hungry' and here we have it, the healthy, instant snack.

Fruit is an excellent convenience food, full of vitamins and nutrients – ready 'packaged' with no cooking or preparation required – just what us busy parents need.

Don't forget about simple juices. If you have a juicer they are fun to make and so healthy and tasty. Skylar and Mia just love helping us choose which combination of fruits and vegetables to use for each juice and then they love drinking it too. Our favourite is carrot, apple and orange – sweet, nutritious and very thirst quenching.

Dairy Products

Dairy produce is available in many forms. It is a very important source of protein (especially for vegetarians who include them in their diet). Children should always have milk of some kind in their diets, whether it is soy (non-dairy), cows', goats', rice milk etc. From the age of one year, until the age of five, children should be given full fat milk because the lower fat types will fill them up without providing all the correct nutrients. By the time they reach five it is okay to give them semi/skimmed milk.

Cheese is also a very popular food with young children. It can be eaten on pasta, in creamy sauces, or simply on its own as a finger food.

Yoghurt is an excellent base to a number of dips and can be eaten as a side dish with almost any meal, and goes particularly well with rice, bean and stewed dishes. It is very nourishing and helps aid digestion. It is rich in A and B vitamins as well as being full of protein and calcium.

Note: Some children are lactose intolerant which means that they cannot have milk or any foods containing milk. If you are unsure of this or have any concerns then please contact your GP.

Non-Dairy Products

These are essential for a vegan diet or a child with a lot of dairy allergies. They are found to be a good source of protein and the best source is soya (or soy) bean. Tofu (made from soya bean curd) is not only high in protein, but also iron and B group vitamins. Even though it is a vegetable based source of iron it is good to include a source of vitamin C in the meal so your body can absorb the iron. Soya products often taste slightly sweeter than dairy products and if possible it is therefore nice to use both to create a variety of flavours.

It is recommended that up until the age of four a child is not given soya products more than once or twice a week.

Eggs

Free range eggs are packed full of calcium, protein and iron, and are an especially important source of these if you are a vegetarian. Once your toddler is over 6 months of age it is okay to give them eggs. They can be made very quickly and are therefore perfect when you are in a rush. My children absolutely love them and here are a few of their favourites. I have even found that serving them boiled eggs with toasted wholemeal soldiers and steamed broccoli florets or steamed asparagus to dip goes down a treat.

Don't forget eggs are brilliant in sandwiches. Simply hard boil an egg, peel it, mash it and mix it with a little mayonnaise and add some chopped cress. You and your toddler can grow cress easily at home on your window sill.

Meat and Fish

Although I am vegetarian, (and always have been) and brought my children up on a vegetarian diet I do understand the importance of meat and fish to some people. High sources of protein and iron and vitamin D (vitamin D is found in particular in oily fish), can be added to and work very well with a number of my recipes as long as the meat is always properly cooked. So adapt my recipes as you please to suit your personal tastes.

Flours

Flours are a good source of proteins and complex carbohydrates. They are available in numerous varieties for example; plain, wholemeal, buckwheat, rice etc. So when using them try to vary the types . Buckwheat flour, high in protein, calcium and iron can be added to cakes, muffins, pancakes and sauces therefore adding higher nutritional value.

Fats and Oils

Fats and oils are important as they contain high levels of vitamins such as A, D and E. Oils high in polyunsaturates such as sunflower, rape seed and ground nut oil are good for general use, whereas oils high in monounsaturates, such as olive oil, are thought to reduce cholesterol levels. I find virgin or extra-virgin olive oil to be a favourite in all my cooking due to its soft flavour.

Herbs and Spices

Herbs are readily available, both fresh and dried. If using dried, freeze-dried is best, otherwise buy in small quantities and

replace regularly. Herbs not only add flavours to an otherwise plain dish, they are also a perfect way to bring out the flavour in a number of dishes without the use of salt. For example add some fresh basil leaves to a simple tomato sauce, it will turn a bland sauce into a delicious dish.

Spices are often thought of as hot and therefore not suitable for young children but this is a misconception. Spices add warmth and colour to meals and your toddler will love the difference they make. Turmeric not only gives a lovely flavour, and a bright yellow colour, it is very good for the immune system. Sweet spices popular with my children are cinnamon and nutmeg.

Spices are fun to experiment with. Add a little to begin with until you know what is right, mix various spices together and you will find combinations your little one likes.

Nuts and Seeds

Nuts and seeds are very versatile and can be crushed or finely ground and added to almost anything, such as stir fries and salads as well as to breads and cakes. In order to obtain the maximum flavour it is useful to lightly roast them first.

But nuts must always be used with caution as they can cause allergies, especially if there is a history of allergy in the family. Likewise oils produced from nuts may cause a reaction, so if you are unsure use an alternative such as olive oil. If you suspect your child may be allergic to something consult your doctor immediately. It is recommended that nuts and seeds should be avoided up to the age of 6 months, and up until 5 years of age be careful with whole nuts in case of choking.

In any case NEVER leave your child unattended whilst eating, in case of choking.

Salt

Babies and young children need little or no salt. Their bodies cannot properly digest it. It can also make your child nervous and irritable.

Children have very acute taste buds, what may appear bland and tasteless to an adult will of consequence be full of flavour to a child. The fresh foods used to make the meals in this book contain enough natural salt themselves. You do not need to add any salt to your children's meals when cooking, or indeed afterwards.

Soups, Dips and Salads

Soups are a brilliant way of getting your child to eat vegetables that they may usually turn their nose up at. Rather than searching for new recipes, try to increase the variety or amount of vegetables added to your favourite family soup recipes. Vegetable soups are great to experiment with as there are just endless combinations of vegetables and herbs to use. A single vegetable is easily disguised in a soup and therefore provides a warming healthy meal, perfect for a cold winter's day or a light lunch at any time of the year.

Kids love dipping things and soup is a great way to make mealtimes fun for them. I usually serve soup to my children with a slice of wholemeal bread and a small piece of cheese to dip. Another good suggestion for soups is to add some pre-cooked small pasta shapes just before serving for a fun addition.

Children who aren't keen on eating cooked vegetables will often eat them raw so try giving them carrot sticks, cucumber, celery, strips of red pepper or cherry tomatoes with a tasty dip. Dips are very handy in that they can be put into small pots or containers, along with some raw vegetables, pita bread or bread sticks and taken anywhere for lunch or simply perhaps as a healthy, tasty snack.

Salads are really quick and easy to create and can be eaten with any other meal or as a lighter lunch on their own, perhaps with some homemade bread. The possibilities are huge from a simple leafy salad to ones with avocado, fish, chicken, potatoes, cheese, nuts, seeds, sprouted seeds and egg, and the great thing about salads is that they are packed full of vitamins and nutrients. They are fresh, you can easily be very imaginative with colours and textures and they can be eaten alongside almost anything.

Chunky Bean Soup

This hearty, wholesome and filling soup uses a vegetable stock which is a great way to use scraps and washed peelings. I find good vegetables to use are onions, garlic, potatoes, sweet potatoes, squash, carrots, celery, mushrooms, peas, corn (even empty corn husks), parsley, green beans, beetroot, bell peppers and don't forget fresh herbs. Serves 3

2 tbsp olive oil
1 small onion, finely chopped
1 garlic clove, crushed
200g tin chopped tomatoes
1 celery stick, finely diced
1 medium carrot, finely diced

250ml vegetable stock (see method below)
Pinch thyme
150g tinned chickpeas, pre-cooked
150g tinned kidney beans, pre-cooked
150g tinned cannellini beans, pre-cooked
Black pepper

1. To make a very easy vegetable stock simply use 300g vegetable ingredients and 800ml water, place everything in a large saucepan and simmer for about 40 minutes. Remove from the heat and strain. Compost the solid ingredients and the liquid is your stock. If you have made a large quantity use what you need and simply freeze the rest in small containers. You can then defrost the required amount next time you need it.

2. In a large saucepan, heat the olive oil, add the onion and garlic and cook for about 5 minutes until soft, but not brown.

3. Add the tomatoes, celery and carrot, stir and then add the vegetable stock and thyme, stir again, cover and simmer for approximately 15 minutes.

4. While this is simmering drain and rinse the beans in cold water. Add to the rest of the ingredients. Allow to simmer for a further 10 minutes, until the beans are hot through. Season with black pepper and serve.

Caitilin's Tip: Instead of using the three separate tins of beans you can use a 200g tin of three bean salad. If your little ones don't like chunky soups then blend the soup to a smoother consistency - it tastes just as good.

Another idea for this recipe is to use less vegetable stock (150ml) and serve it as a stew with some dumplings (recipe page 25).

Courgette and Carrot Soup

This sweet, bright, fresh and yummy meal is rich in iron and vitamins A and C. Perfect eaten with some buttered, soft, warm fresh bread (recipe page 72).
Serves 3

1 tbsp olive oil
1 onion, sliced
1 garlic clove, crushed
1 medium courgette, grated

2 large carrots, grated
600ml water
50ml full cream milk
1 tbsp fresh basil, chopped

1. Heat the oil in a thick-based pan, add the onion and garlic and cook gently until softened, for about 5 minutes.

2. Add the grated courgette and carrots, stirring them in the oil for 2-3 minutes.

3. Add the water and bring to the boil, cover and simmer for 10-15 minutes.

4. Remove from the heat, add the milk and blend to a creamy consistency.

5. Stir in the chopped basil and serve.

Creamy Leek and Potato Soup

A light, creamy and delicious soup. Children may think they don't like leeks, but this is a brilliant recipe for disguising them – they won't even realise they are eating them. Serves 4

3 medium potatoes, peeled and diced
600ml vegetable stock
1 small onion, chopped

1 medium leek, chopped
150ml full cream milk
Pinch fresh parsley, finely chopped

1. Put the potatoes into a medium sized saucepan with the vegetable stock, cover and bring to the boil. Turn down the heat and simmer for 10 minutes.

2. Add the onion and leek to the pan and continue to simmer for a further 10–15 minutes, or until the vegetables are soft.

3. Remove from the heat and add the milk. Put it all in a blender and combine until smooth. Pour back into a saucepan and stir in the chopped parsley.

4. Allow to cool and serve with fresh bread or dumplings.

Hearty Lentil Soup

A number of friends bring their children to my house just so they can have my soup for lunch and this soup is and has always been a huge favourite. It is high in protein and fibre and enriched with vitamins A, B and C. Serves 4

175g dried continental (green) lentils
1 small onion, peeled and diced
1 garlic clove, crushed
1 tbsp olive oil
1 medium carrot, peeled and grated
2 button mushrooms, chopped

1 celery stick, chopped
50g sweetcorn
200g tin chopped tomatoes
300ml water
200ml full cream milk
Pinch marjoram

1. Rinse the lentils, put in a pan and cover with cold water. Cover the pan and bring to the boil. Boil rapidly for 10 minutes, reduce the heat and simmer for a further 35 minutes or until tender. If they go slightly dry when they are cooking add more boiling water (do not allow to boil dry or they will burn).

Whilst the lentils are cooking prepare and cook the remaining ingredients.

2. In a large heavy bottomed saucepan gently fry the onion and garlic in the olive oil for 1-2 minutes, add the carrot, mushrooms, celery and sweetcorn and cook for a further 5 minutes until slightly soft.

3. Add the tomatoes, stir, cover with a lid and simmer for a further 10-15 minutes. Stir regularly to ensure the vegetables don't stick to the bottom of the saucepan.

4. When the lentils are soft add them to the cooked vegetables. At this point add a further 300ml water and the marjoram. Stir and simmer for a further 10-15 minutes, this way all the juices will be absorbed and the flavours will combine.

5. Remove from the heat add the milk and purée until smooth.

6. Allow to cool and serve.

Caitilin's Tip: You can use red split lentils, they will cook more quickly and the finished soup will be a warm orangey colour instead of brown.

As the recipe makes a surplus you can freeze it and use at a later date either for soup, or as a bolognese or a pie filling, the options are endless.

Pea, Leek and Broccoli Soup

An excellent soup for disguising green vegetables and perfect when eaten with nice warm crusty bread or some homemade croutons. Serves 4

2 tbsp olive oil
1 garlic clove, crushed
2 medium sized leeks, chopped
2 medium potatoes, peeled and diced
250ml vegetable stock (recipe page 18)

100g broccoli florets, roughly chopped
50g frozen peas
2 tbsp fresh parsley, chopped
Freshly ground black pepper

1. In a large pan heat the olive oil and gently sauté the garlic and leeks for approximately 10 minutes, until soft but do not allow them to go brown.

2. Add the potatoes and vegetable stock, stir, bring to the boil, cover and reduce to a simmer for about 10 minutes. Add the broccoli and peas and simmer for a further 10 minutes until the vegetables are soft.

3. Remove from the heat put in a blender and blend to a creamy consistency, add the parsley and black pepper. Re-heat slowly if necessary and serve.

Tomato Soup

A tasty soup with a vibrant colour that will appeal to any inquisitive toddler. Rich in vitamin A and C, it has a slightly sweet flavour and works well with fresh bread soldiers, cheese, and even carrot sticks. Serves 4

1 small onion, finely chopped
1 garlic clove, crushed
2 tbsp olive oil
600g fresh tomatoes (about 7 medium tomatoes), skinned and diced

150ml water
150ml full cream milk
Pinch fresh basil, finely chopped

1. Gently fry the onion and garlic in the olive oil for 5 minutes.

2. Skin the tomatoes (see below) and dice the flesh. Add to the onion and garlic and stir. Add the water, stir, cover and simmer for 15 minutes, until the tomatoes have broken down.

3. Remove from the heat, add the milk and blend to a smooth consistency.

4. Add the finely chopped basil and stir. Allow to cool before serving.

Caitilin's Tip: To skin the tomatoes simply drop them into boiling water for approximately 10 seconds, remove carefully from the water. Pierce them and the skins will easily come away. You don't have to remove the skins, but when they are blended you will not have such a smooth consistency, so it depends what your child likes.

Watercress Soup

This bright green soup is full of iron, vitamin C, zinc, and folic acid - all enhancing the immune system. Serve with some garlic bread or herby garlic croutons. Serves 2

1 tbsp olive oil
1 garlic clove, crushed
1 small leek or 1 small onion, chopped
1 medium potato, peeled and diced

250ml water, boiling
150ml full cream milk
85g watercress, washed and chopped

1. In a large pan heat the olive oil and gently sauté the garlic and leek or onion for approximately 10 minutes, do not allow it to go brown.

2. Add the potato and the boiling water, stir, bring back to the boil, cover and reduce to a simmer for about 15 minutes, until the potato is soft.

3. Add the milk and watercress, bring to the boil and remove from the heat.

4. Blend to a creamy consistency, re-heat slowly if necessary and serve.

Herby Garlic Croutons

Your little ones can help you make these croutons and then count them into their soup before fishing them out again and into their mouths. Serves 1

1 slice brown or wholemeal bread
Small knob unsalted butter

1/2 small garlic clove, crushed
Pinch mixed herbs

1. Pre-heat the oven to 180°C, gas 4.

2. Mash the butter with the crushed garlic and herbs in a small dish.

3. Lightly toast the bread and spread on the garlic butter evenly.

4. Cut into small squares (1cm) and spread on a baking tray.

5. Put in the pre-heated oven for approximately 10 minutes, until the bread has crisped and browned. Remove and serve in a soup.

Dumplings

Dumplings are brilliant added to soups and stews, giving a lovely texture and flavour. Kids like to explore with their food and my children love 'fishing' for the dumplings. Serves 2-3

60g plain flour
1 tsp baking powder
1/2 tsp paprika
Pinch parsley

1/2 tsp mixed herbs
1 tbsp vegetable suet
4 tbsp water

1. Sift the flour, baking powder and paprika into a medium sized mixing bowl.

2. Using a metal spoon stir in the herbs and suet.

3. Bind together with the water to form a soft dough.

4. Divide into 10 portions and roll gently in your hands to form small balls.

5. Add to the soup or stew and allow to simmer for 15 minutes, stir so that they don't stick to the bottom of the pan – they will bob to the surface and float as they cook.

Butter Bean and Herb Dip

A creamy fresh dip full of protein, fibre, potassium, iron and vitamin B and your children won't even realise they are eating beans. It tastes especially good when served with fresh vegetable sticks such as carrots, sweet peppers and cucumber. Serves 4

200g tin butter beans, drained and rinsed
100g plain cottage cheese

1 tbsp mayonnaise
1 tbsp fresh mixed herbs, chopped

1. Put all the ingredients into a food processor and purée to a smooth consistency.
2. Remove from the blender and put in a small bowl, cover and put in the fridge and leave to chill for at least 30 minutes before serving.

Cream Cheese and Chive Dip

A really simple and yummy dip rich in calcium and vitamin D. It is perfect as a quick snack for those in-between-meal hungry moments or even in a sandwich as part of a healthy lunch. Serves 3-4

4 tbsp cream cheese
Small bunch fresh chives

Sprig fresh parsley, finely chopped
Freshly ground black pepper (optional)

1. Put the cream cheese into a small bowl and mash until completely smooth.
2. Chop the chives and parsley finely and mix them into the cream cheese. Add the black pepper and mix well.
3. Serve as a dip with some raw vegetables or herby potato wedges (page 48) or as a simple sandwich filler.

Guacamole

Avocados are an excellent source of vitamin E. Soft and creamy in texture with a slight nutty flavour, they make an excellent base for this dip. The yoghurt gives it a light and smoother texture. Serves 4

1 ripe avocado
1/2 small garlic clove, crushed
1 tbsp fresh lemon juice

1 fresh tomato, skinned
3 tbsp natural plain yoghurt

1. Peel the avocado and remove the stone from the centre, place in a blender and whiz for 30 seconds.

2. Add the crushed garlic, lemon juice and skinned tomato (tip page 23) and purée for a further minute until all the ingredients are nicely combined.

3. Remove from the blender, put into a bowl and stir in the yoghurt.

4. Serve immediately. Excellent with bread sticks or raw vegetable strips.

Hummus

Hummus has always been a favourite with my children; used as a dip or in sandwiches, they never tire of it. The secret of good hummus is the tahini (sesame seed paste), which is readily available in supermarkets and health food shops. Serves 4

400g tin chickpeas, drained
2 tbsp tahini
Juice of 1 lemon

1/2 garlic clove, crushed
4 tbsp cold water

1. Put the chickpeas, tahini, lemon juice, garlic and water into a blender or food processor and mix into a smooth paste. If it is very thick and hard to blend then add extra water.

2. Spoon the hummus into a bowl and serve.

Caitilin's Tip: It can be stored in an airtight container in the fridge for up to 4 days.

Tsatsiki

My children love this dip served with their meals, especially rice or other grain based dishes. Cucumbers are very good sources of vitamin C, vitamin K, and potassium. Serves 2

¼ cucumber, peeled or washed and diced very small

6 tbsp natural plain yoghurt
Freshly ground black pepper (optional)

1. Mix all the ingredients in a small bowl, chill in the fridge and serve.

Caitilin's Tip: **Minty yoghurt is a variation. Simply grind three fresh mint leaves, or if you don't have a herb grinder then chop it very finely and stir it into 6 tbsp of natural plain yoghurt with 1 tsp freshly squeezed lime juice.**

Avocado Bowls and Cottage Cheese

Avocados are a complete food, with fourteen minerals to stimulate growth, including iron and copper. Skylar and Mia love this instant snack because they can scoop the cottage cheese and fleshy avocado straight from its skin. Serves 1

½ ripe avocado, de-stoned
2 tsp cottage cheese
For the dressing
100ml olive oil

Juice of 1 lemon
1 tsp salt
1 tsp runny honey
1 tsp caster sugar

1. To make the dressing put all the ingredients in a small jug or dressing bottle and mix well until all the ingredients are combined.

2. Put the avocado on a dish and spoon the cottage cheese into the hole left by the stone and drizzle with French dressing.

Caitilin's Tip: **To make a spicier dressing add 1 tsp wholegrain French mustard.**

Bulgur and Broad Bean Salad

Bulgur (also known as cracked wheat) is very easy to cook, similar to couscous. It is an excellent source of complex carbohydrates and also a useful source of B vitamins. Serves 3

450ml water
150g bulgur (cracked wheat)
30g fresh broad beans
   (frozen work just as well)
4 cherry tomatoes, diced

2 tbsp fresh basil leaves
1 tbsp olive oil
2 tbsp lemon juice
Freshly ground black pepper to taste

1. Bring the water to a boil in a medium sized saucepan. Add the bulgur and simmer for 15-20 minutes or until the water is absorbed and the bulgur is soft.

2. Cook the broad beans in a separate pan of boiling water; 10 minutes for fresh or 5 minutes for frozen. Drain.

3. Spoon the bulgur into a medium sized bowl and allow to cool.

4. Combine the remaining ingredients with the bulgur. Mix well and serve.

Couscous Salad

Couscous, which is so quick and easy to cook, bulks out this salad and provides an essential carbohydrate to a nutritious meal. Serves 2

150ml water
20g French beans, chopped
75g couscous
2 tsp sunflower seeds
6 cherry tomatoes, quartered
1 tbsp lemon juice

Small bunch chives, chopped
2 tsp fresh parsley, chopped
1/2 little gem lettuce, washed and torn
Red Leicester cheese, finely grated,
 to garnish (optional)

1. Bring the water to a boil in a small saucepan, add the French beans. Cover and allow to simmer for 10 minutes, until the beans are soft.

2. Turn off the heat and add the couscous and sunflower seeds, stir and cover for 9 minutes.

3. When all the water has been absorbed by the couscous fluff the grains with a fork and gently stir in the cherry tomatoes, lemon juice, chives and parsley.

4. Arrange the lettuce in a shallow dish and spoon the couscous salad over the top. Sprinkle with a little finely grated cheese if desired.

Caitilin's Tip: **Add 2 tbsp sprouted seeds, such as sprouted alfalfa, or sprouted sunflower seeds to the salad. They add a delicious and nutritious crunch.**

Greek Salad

Both my daughters have always loved this simple and nutritious combination of mild cheese and juicy, crunchy vegetables and would probably eat it every day if they could. Serves 2

1/4 cucumber, peeled or washed, diced
2 large ripe tomatoes, washed and roughly chopped
1/4 packet feta cheese, crumbled

16 pitted or pimento stuffed green olives, rinsed
1 tbsp olive oil
1 tbsp wine vinegar

1. In a large bowl, toss together cucumber, tomatoes, feta cheese, and green olives.

2. Whisk together the oil and vinegar and just before serving drizzle this over the salad, tossing it together.

Stripy Rainbow Salad

A bright and fun dish which your children will love. Take them shopping with you to help pick out the brightly coloured vegetables. Beetroot is high in fibre with a lovely sweet flavour. Carrots complement this and are an excellent source of vitamins A, B and C. Serves 2

1 carrot, peeled and finely sliced into 3cm strips
2 cooked beetroots, finely sliced into 3cm strips
1/2 sweet red pepper, finely sliced into 3cm strips
1/2 sweet orange pepper, finely sliced into 3cm strips
1 tbsp freshly squeezed lemon juice

1. Toss all the vegetables together in a medium sized bowl, stir in the lemon juice and serve.

Lemon Courgette Salad

I came across this recipe when I was in France one summer and I thought it sounded really strange to be eating raw courgette. I was surprised however to find it absolutely delicious and the bonus was so did my children. Courgettes are packed full of potassium, and vitamins A and C and they are very tender vegetables with a fresh, delicate flavour which is why they work perfectly in this very simple salad. Serves 2

2 medium sized courgettes, sliced very finely with a peeler
1 lemon, squeezed

20g fresh Parmesan cheese, shaved
Freshly ground black pepper

1. Put the sliced courgettes in a large mixing bowl, pour on the lemon juice and mix well so all of the courgette slices are covered with the juice.

2. Put this in the refrigerator for at least an hour to marinate. The lemon juice will 'cook' the courgettes.

3. Remove from the refrigerator and stir, add the shaved Parmesan and freshly ground black pepper.

Caitilin's Tip: **This tastes great on a summer's day as an accompaniment to a BBQ.**

Pasta, Vegetables, Grains and Bakes

Any one of these ingredients should and probably will form the basis to a healthy and nutritious meal, either eaten together such as pasta with a vegetable based sauce, a risotto served with a simple portion of vegetables, or perhaps simply a boiled egg with soldiers or asparagus to dip, the list of wonderful tempting dishes is endless.

Pasta, a firm favourite with my children combined with a simple and nutritious sauce, is a brilliant no hassle meal – just what us parents are looking for.

Vegetables are packed full of important vitamins and minerals, either eaten raw with a dip or as a salad, or cooked in a sauce or bake. Involve your children here, take them shopping and let them choose, count the vegetables together and look at all the beautiful shapes and array of colours. If they do this simple shopping task with you they are much more likely to want to eat it later on.

Once your toddler is over 6 months of age it is okay to give them eggs. They involve little preparation, cook quickly and are therefore perfect when you are in a rush, or get home later than expected and don't have much time to cook.

Grains are not only a very important source of energy, carbohydrate, protein and fibre, but are cheap to buy, versatile, fun and quick to cook.

Bakes, which include a simple pie or a non-pastry based dish such as cheesy broccoli bake, are a brilliant way of incorporating different vegetables together. Children and adults will love and enjoy the following of my family favourites together.

Asparagus Risotto

A very simple and fun way to incorporate different vegetables into a dish which everyone likes – rice. **Serves 3**

400g fresh asparagus, chopped
1 small onion, chopped
2 tbsp olive oil
150g arborio rice
600ml vegetable stock (page 18)
30g peas

50g freshly grated Parmesan cheese
  (if you don't have this then ordinary
  cheddar cheese is fine)
2 tbsp fresh chopped parsley
Ground black pepper to season

1. Cut the tough ends off the stems of the asparagus and cut into 2.5cm pieces, put aside. Chop the onion.

2. Heat the olive oil in a large saucepan over medium heat. Sauté the onion for 5 minutes until soft, not brown. Stir in the dry rice.

3. Cook for 1 minute, stirring together.

4. Add the vegetable stock and peas. Bring the rice to a boil, turn down the heat and cook for 10 minutes stirring frequently. Add the asparagus and continue to cook for a further 20 minutes, stirring all the time. The rice will become sticky and soft.

5. Remove the pan from the heat and stir in the Parmesan cheese, parsley and ground pepper.

Caitilin's Tip: When ready the risotto will have a creamy sauce. Serve with some natural plain yoghurt and a simple salad.

Egg Paella

Rice is always a good base to a healthy meal. In this recipe all the goodness from the fresh vegetables and protein from the egg is incorporated into a simple, yet colourful and tasty dish that the whole family can enjoy. **Serves 4**

2 medium size eggs
2 tbsp olive oil
1 small onion, chopped
1 garlic clove, crushed
3 tablespoons olive oil
1/2 medium sweet red pepper, de-seeded
   and chopped

250g tinned chopped tomatoes
40g sweet corn
40g peas
1/2 tsp turmeric
150g long grain rice
300ml water
Pinch mixed herbs to season

1. Bring a small saucepan of water to the boil and add the eggs, turn down the heat and allow to boil gently for 10 minutes, this length of time will ensure that they are hard boiled. When they are cooked remove from the boiling water and run under cold water while removing the shell. Set aside.

2. While the eggs are cooking put the onion, garlic and olive oil in a medium saucepan, fry gently for 5 minutes, until softened slightly.

3. Add the red pepper, tomatoes, sweet corn and peas to the cooking onion and garlic, mix and cook for a further 3-4 minutes.

4. Add the turmeric, rice and water, stir and bring to the boil. Cover and allow to simmer for a further 15-20 minutes, until the rice is soft and all the water has been absorbed.

5. Cut the eggs into roughly 2cm pieces and add to the rice, gently mix in and serve.

Caitilin's Tip: Serve with soy sauce sprinkled on top and some fresh purple sprouted broccoli and some plain natural yoghurt on the side.

Roasted Squashy Rice

This sweet, bright and colourful rice dish is a favourite with my family. The squash adds a natural sweetness and soft texture. **Serves 4**

6 tbsp olive oil, for frying and roasting
1/2 small butternut squash, peeled and
   diced (2cm cubes)
1 small onion, chopped
1 garlic clove, crushed
1/2 sweet red pepper, diced
10 small button mushrooms, chopped
3 large tomatoes, skinned and diced

20g sweet corn
20g garden peas
50g long grain rice
1 tsp turmeric
450ml boiling water
Pinch fresh chives, finely chopped
Pinch fresh oregano, finely chopped

1. Pre-heat the oven to 220°C, gas 7.

2. The squash must be roasted first as this takes the longest to cook. Put 4 tbsp of the olive oil into a roasting tin. Put the diced squash into the tin, toss in the olive oil and put into the pre-heated oven. Roast for approximately 30 minutes, or until the squash is soft. Turn occasionally to ensure all sides get cooked.

While it is roasting you can prepare and cook the rest of the dish.

3. Heat the remainder of the olive oil in a large saucepan and add the onion and garlic and cook for 5 minutes until soft.

4. Add the red pepper, mushrooms and tomatoes, stir and cook gently for 2-3 minutes.

5. Add the sweet corn, peas, rice and turmeric. Stir and cook for a further minute.

6. Add the water and bring to the boil. Stirring frequently, simmer for a further 10-12 minutes or until most of the liquid has been absorbed and the rice is soft.

7. Remove the squash from the oven and stir it into the rice. Add the herbs, stir and allow to cool slightly before serving.

Caitilin's Tip: My children love this delicious rice dish served with a simple salad and some natural organic plain yoghurt.

Cool Arrabiata

My husband originally taught me how to make this pasta dish. Traditionally it's spicy, made with chilli pepper and ginger, but I adapted it to suit my children and they love it this way. **Serves 2**

200g spaghetti
1 tbsp olive oil
1 garlic clove, crushed
1 small carrot, peeled and grated
1/2 courgette, grated
200g tinned chopped tomatoes

Pinch dried or fresh marjoram
  (if fresh finely chopped)
1 tbsp freshly squeezed lemon juice
2 tbsp natural full fat yoghurt
Grated cheese to serve

1. Bring a large saucepan of water to boil, add the pasta and cook on a rolling boil for about 15 minutes until soft.

2. While the pasta is cooking make the sauce. In a small saucepan add the olive oil, garlic, carrot and courgette, cook over a moderate heat for 4-5 minutes, add the chopped tomatoes and marjoram and allow to simmer for 15 minutes, until the sauce has reduced. Stir frequently to stop the sauce from sticking to the saucepan.

3. Remove from the heat. Stir in the lemon juice and yoghurt.

4. Stir into the drained pasta and serve with a little grated cheese on top.

Caitilin's Tip: If you want a more spicy meal simply add a chopped fresh chilli pepper and 1/2 tsp of chopped ginger when you fry the garlic.

Macaroni Cheese with Trees

This recipe is based on a traditional macaroni cheese, but I have adapted it to Skylar and Mia's tastes to include more protein and vitamins A, C and D. This recipe makes enough for the whole family to enjoy. **Serves 3**

200g macaroni
6 large broccoli florets, roughly chopped
1 medium egg

For the sauce
300ml organic semi-skimmed milk

3 level tbsp plain flour
25g unsalted butter
25g Cheddar cheese, grated
1 tbsp parsley, finely chopped
20g extra Cheddar cheese (optional)
30g breadcrumbs (optional)

1. Bring a medium sized saucepan of water to the boil, add the macaroni and bring back to the boil. Turn down the heat, cover with a lid and allow to cook on a rolling boil for 10-15 minutes (timings depend on the macaroni used – check the packet), until soft.

2. After the macaroni has been cooking for 5 minutes add the broccoli florets and continue to boil.

3. Put the egg in boiling water in a separate small saucepan, cover and boil for 10 minutes (so it is hardboiled).

4. While this is cooking make the sauce. Put the milk, flour and butter into a saucepan, over a medium heat. Stir continuously with a whisk (this will ensure it doesn't get lumpy) for about 5-10 minutes until the mixture thickens.

5. Add the grated cheese and parsley, and stir. The cheese will slightly thicken the mixture.

6. By now the macaroni and broccoli should be cooked. Remove from the heat, and drain off the water and put the pasta back into the saucepan.

7. Remove the shell from the egg and cut roughly into chunks. Put this and the cheese sauce onto the macaroni and stir the whole lot together.

You can now either serve it like this, or pour it all into an ovenproof dish, cover with a small amount of extra grated cheese or breadcrumbs, bake for 10 minutes in a moderate pre-heated oven (190°C, gas 5) until it is slightly browned, remove from the oven and allow to cool slightly before giving it to your children as it will be very hot.

Rainbow Spaghetti

Brightly coloured vegetables are the most nutritious; the pigment that gives them their colour also contains vital nutrients. In this recipe they make a very simple but tasty sauce for pasta. Serves 2

200g spaghetti

For the sauce
1 small onion, diced
2 tbsp olive oil
1/2 small courgette, diced
1 small carrot, peeled and diced

30g sweet corn
400g tinned chopped tomatoes
Pinch dried oregano to season
Pinch basil to season, finely chopped

Small amount of grated Cheddar or
    Parmesan cheese to serve

1. To make the sauce fry the onion in the olive oil in a small saucepan for 3 minutes, add the diced vegetables and the chopped tomatoes, stir and allow to simmer. Stir regularly to ensure it doesn't stick, for approximately 15 minutes, until the sauce has reduced and the vegetables are soft. Add the oregano and basil, stir in and remove from the heat. While the sauce is cooking boil the spaghetti.

4. Bring a large saucepan of water to boil, add the spaghetti, cover, turn down the heat and cook on a rolling boil for approximately 10-12 minutes, until soft.

3. Drain the water from the spaghetti and serve with a large spoonful of sauce and grated cheese on top.

There is enough sauce for more than one meal, so simply put the surplus in an airtight container and refrigerate (keep for 3 days), or freeze, it lasts much longer this way.

Tomato Sauce with Secret Vegetables

This is the perfect pasta sauce for children who aren't keen on vegetables. By using this recipe you can easily disguise lots of very healthy nutritious vegetables in it. **Serves 2-3**

1 small onion, diced
1 garlic clove, crushed
1 small carrot, peeled and grated
1/2 small courgette, diced

25g sweet corn
3 button mushrooms, chopped
400g tinned chopped tomatoes
Fresh basil, finely chopped

1. In a small saucepan fry the onion and crushed garlic for 2-3 minutes, so they are just warmed through.

2. Add the remaining vegetables and chopped tomatoes. Simmer over a moderate heat for 10-15 minutes, until the vegetables are soft and the tomato juice has reduced down.

3. Remove from the heat and purée to a smooth consistency.

4. Finally stir in the chopped basil.

Caitilin's Tip: Serve with any variety of pasta or even rice.

Baby Vegetables and Tofu with Rice Noodles

Kids love baby vegetables, they are just the right size and are full of essential vitamins and nutrients. The tofu is soft and very tasty; adding protein and calcium to this quick and easy meal. **Serves 3**

3 tbsp soy sauce
1 garlic clove, crushed
2 tbsp runny honey
3 tbsp lemon juice
100g plain firm tofu, cut into small chunks
2 tbsp olive oil
50g asparagus, chopped

50g baby sweet corn, chopped
40g mangetout peas
40g French beans, chopped
1 medium carrot, sliced into 3cm strips
40g bean sprouts
200g rice noodles

1. In a small bowl combine the soy sauce, crushed garlic, honey and lemon juice.

2. Add the tofu to this marinade and allow to marinate for at least half an hour.

3. Heat the olive oil in a wok (if you don't have one a large frying pan will do).

4. Add the vegetables and tofu and stir fry for 5-10 minutes. While this is cooking cook the rice noodles. Put them in a medium sized bowl and pour over boiling water, making sure the noodles are completely covered. Leave to stand for 5 minutes, or until soft.

5. Drain the noodles and add them to the vegetables, cook for a further 3-5 minutes until the noodles have cooked with the vegetables and have absorbed some of the flavours from the sauce.

6. Serve immediately.

Caitilin's Tip: You could stir in cooked diced chicken to this recipe when the vegetables are added.

Roast Vegetable Lasagne

Lasagne is easily prepared in advance and is perfect for the whole family, everyone will love this one. Serves 4

6 lasagne sheets
50g mozzarella, grated
1 small onion, chopped
1 garlic clove, crushed
1/2 aubergine, diced
200g cherry tomatoes, halved
1 small courgette, diced
1/2 sweet red pepper, diced
40g sweet corn

fresh basil, torn

For the cheese sauce
300ml milk
3 tbsp plain flour
25g unsalted butter
grating of fresh nutmeg
20g Cheddar cheese
Extra grated cheese for the top

1. Pre-heat the oven to 220°C, gas 7.

2. Arrange all the vegetables, including the onion and crushed garlic in a large baking tray and drizzle with the olive oil. Turn so the oil is coating the vegetables.

3. Place the tray at the top of the pre-heated oven and cook for 30 minutes until the vegetables have browned at the edges and are soft. While this is cooking make the cheese sauce.

4. Combine the milk, flour and butter in a saucepan and stir continuously using a whisk (this will ensure it doesn't get lumpy) over a moderate heat until the mixture thickens. If required add more milk, this will thin down the sauce.

5. Add the nutmeg and grated Cheddar cheese, stir into the sauce.

6. Remove the vegetables from the oven and turn down the heat to 190°C, gas 5.

7. Cover the base of a large 23cm x 23cm x 5cm ovenproof dish with a quarter of the cheese sauce.

8. On top of that put a layer of 2 lasagne sheets. Cover with half of the vegetable mixture and put half of the grated mozzarella on top of the vegetables. Repeat this and finally lay the third layer of lasagne sheets on top and cover with the remaining cheese sauce.

9. Cover with some extra grated cheese.

10. Put near the top of a pre-heated oven for 30-40 minutes, until the top has browned and the lasagne sheets are cooked through. You can test this by inserting a clean knife and if it feels soft it is ready.

Caitilin's Tip: Serve with a crunchy salad..

Chickpea and Aubergine Stew

Chickpeas are a great source of calcium, zinc, and protein. They are also very high in dietary fibre and therefore are a healthy food source. In this delicious stew they are combined with aubergines in a simple tomato sauce. **Serves 3**

1 tbsp olive oil
1 small onion, finely chopped
1 garlic clove, crushed
1 small aubergine, diced

6 button mushrooms, sliced
250g tinned chickpeas
400g tin chopped tomatoes
Mixed herbs to season

1. Slowly fry the onion, garlic, aubergine and mushrooms in the oil for approximately 5 minutes, until softened.

2. Add the remaining ingredients and stir well.

3. Allow to simmer for 15 minutes over a medium heat, stirring frequently to ensure the stew doesn't stick to the base of the saucepan and burn.

4. Serve with some rice or simple couscous and plain natural yoghurt.

Creamy Beetroot in a Potato Boat

This is a very inexpensive recipe that not only tastes good but has a great colour as well. **Serves 4**

2 tbsp olive oil
1 small onion, finely chopped
4 mushrooms, sliced
2 tbsp plain white flour
150ml whole milk
250g cooked beetroot, sliced

For the potato boat
3 medium sized potatoes, peeled and diced
4 tbsp whole milk
10g butter
Freshly ground black pepper, to season

1. Bring a large saucepan of water to the boil and put the potatoes in, cover and allow to boil for 20 minutes until they are soft.

2. While the potatoes are cooking pre-heat the oven to 200°C, gas 6 and prepare the beetroot part of the dish. In a medium sized saucepan heat the olive oil and add the onion and mushrooms, gently cook them for 5 minutes, until soft.

3. Add the flour and milk to the saucepan and stir continuously to prevent the sauce getting lumpy.

4. Add the sliced cooked beetroot, stir, cook for a further 5 minutes, remove from the heat and put aside.

5. By now the potatoes will be soft so remove them from the heat and drain. Add the milk and butter and mash until they are soft and fluffy.

6. Put the mashed potato in a round serving dish and make a well in the centre.

7. Spoon the prepared beetroot into this well. Grate some cheese on the top and warm through in the pre-heated oven until the cheese has melted and browned.

Creamy Spinach Mash

If your toddler loves mashed potato but won't touch spinach then this is the perfect recipe for you. The finely chopped spinach is disguised in the potato – it makes the potato green but just explain it's magic green potato. **Serves 2**

3 medium sized potatoes,
   peeled and diced
50g fresh spinach, washed

3 tbsp whole milk
10g butter
Freshly ground black pepper, to season

1. Bring a large saucepan of water to the boil and add the potatoes. Cover and boil for 20 minutes until they are soft.

2. While the potatoes are cooking steam the spinach over the boiling potatoes. If you don't have a steamer then cooking it separately in a little water is fine.

3. When the potatoes are soft remove them from the heat and drain. Add the milk and butter and mash until they are soft and fluffy. Add a small amount of black pepper to season.

4. Squeeze any excess water from the spinach and finely chop, mash in with the potato and serve.

Crispy Sweet Vegetable Medley

The deep orange of a sweet potato contains more nutrients than an ordinary potato and combined with parsnips they make a yummy nutritious alternative to roast potatoes. **Serves 2**

1 medium sweet potato, peeled and chopped
1 parsnip, peeled and chopped
1 red onion, halved and split

1/2 sweet red pepper, roughly chopped
2 sprigs fresh thyme
4 tbsp olive oil

1. Pre-heat the oven to 230°C, gas 8.

2. Put the vegetables in a deep baking tray or roasting tin with the sprigs of thyme and toss in the olive so it coats them.

3. Put into the pre-heated oven and roast for approximately 25-30 minutes, turning regularly until all sides are nicely browned and the vegetables are soft.

4. Remove from the oven and serve with a selection of any vegetables, a BBQ or simply with a meal of your choice.

Caitilin's Tip: Add some butternut squash to the tray and roast them as well. Sweet potatoes are delicious with an amazing texture and they are a very nutritious vegetable on their own. Try baking them whole in a hot (230°C, gas 8) oven for about 30-40 minutes and serve sliced in half with some butter and grated cheese.

Gamps' Potato Latkes

My grandfather used to come over from America every year and make these for us. They are crispy on the outside and tender on the inside, yummy served with a simple apple sauce and a side salad. **Serves 4**

200ml vegetable or sunflower oil,
  for frying
3 large potatoes, peeled and grated

1 small onion, grated
1 egg, beaten
3 tbsp plain flour

1. Combine all the ingredients together in a large mixing bowl.

Heat the vegetable oil (1-2cm deep) in a frying pan. When the oil is really hot take one tablespoon of the mixture at a time and place in the hot oil, press them down to form patties 1.5cm thick. You can fit a number of these into the pan at a time. **Keep your children well away from the hot oil, as it can spit and be very dangerous.**

4. Turn the latkes so they are evenly cooked and nicely browned.

3. Remove from the pan and drain on some kitchen towel before serving.

Garlic Mushrooms

A very quick and easy mushroom recipe that goes really well with some simple mashed potato and broccoli. **Serves 2**

6 button mushrooms, chopped
1 garlic clove, crushed
1 small knob butter

1/2 tsp mixed herbs, dried
Freshly ground pepper, to season

1. Melt the butter in a small saucepan, add the chopped mushrooms and crushed garlic. Stir and cover.

2. Add the mixed herbs and black pepper, allow the mushrooms to cook very slowly over a low heat for approximately 5 minutes until soft, stirring regularly.

3. Remove from the heat and serve with the juices.

Herby Potato Wedges

My husband came up with these after a long summer of BBQs. They are very versatile and are the perfect healthy alternative to chips and can be served with almost anything. So enjoy them with your little one – we certainly do. **Serves 3**

4 medium potatoes
3 tbsp olive oil
1 garlic clove, finely chopped

1 tsp mixed herbs to season
Freshly ground black pepper

1. Pre-heat the oven to 200°C, gas 6.

2. Thoroughly wash the potatoes, cut in half and then into slices 5mm thick.

3. Spread the olive oil evenly over a baking tray, put the potatoes in the tray and toss them in the oil to coat them.

4. Sprinkle the garlic, herbs and the black pepper over the potatoes.

5. Put them at the top of the hot oven and allow to cook for 30-40 minutes, until soft. Turn them regularly using a spatula, so both sides cook and they do not burn or stick to the baking tray.

6. Carefully remove from the oven and serve.

Mild Creamy Curry

Children will love this curry for its sweet flavour and mild taste. Very nutritious and works really well with some rice and plain natural yoghurt. **Serves 4**

2 medium sized potatoes, peeled and
    diced
2 tbsp olive oil
1 small onion, chopped
1 garlic clove, crushed
1/2 tsp ground cumin
1/2 tsp garam masala
1 tsp turmeric

1/2 butternut squash, peeled and diced
5 mushrooms, chopped
2 tbsp pumpkin seeds
250ml coconut milk
20g peas
20g sweet corn
100g fresh spinach, washed

1. Bring a large saucepan of water to the boil and add the potatoes, cover and boil for 5 minutes. Remove from the heat, drain and put to one side.

2. Heat the oil in a large saucepan and add the onion, garlic and spices, cook for 2-3 minutes and add the partially cooked potatoes, butternut squash, mushrooms and pumpkin seeds. Stir and add the coconut milk.

3. Cover and allow to simmer for 20 minutes, stirring frequently to ensure it doesn't stick to the base of the pan.

4. Add the peas, sweet corn and spinach, stir and allow to cook for a further 10 minutes, until all the vegetables are soft.

Caitilin's Tip: Make double the quantity and freeze the extra.

Ratatouille

A lovely bright, quick and easy meal, packed with essential vitamins. It is perfect eaten with a carbohydrate such as rice or potatoes. **Serves 2**

½ small onion, finely sliced
1 tbsp olive oil, for frying
1 tsp tomato purée
1 small carrot, peeled and finely sliced
½ small courgette, sliced into rounds

20g sweet corn
200g tinned chopped tomatoes
Fresh mixed herbs to season, finely
chopped

1. Gently fry the finely sliced onion in the olive oil for 2-3 minutes, add the tomato purée and stir. Cook for a further minute.

2. Add the carrot and courgette, stir and allow to cook for 5 minutes before adding the chopped tomatoes and sweet corn.

3. Mix it all together, cover and cook over a medium heat for a further 10 minutes, or until the carrot is soft. Finely chop the fresh mixed herbs and stir in at the end so the flavour is kept. Allow to cool and serve.

Stir Fried Vegetables with Cashew Nuts

Stir fries are one of the quickest meals to make, requiring very little cooking they remain crunchy, bright in colour and very nutritious. The added nuts in this recipe can be omitted if you or your children have a nut allergy. **Serves 2**

For the sauce
1 garlic clove, crushed
1/2 lemon, squeezed
1/4 tsp Chinese 5 spice
3 tbsp soy sauce
2 tbsp runny honey

3 tbsp olive oil
1 carrot, peeled and thinly sliced
3 tbsp red or white cabbage, shredded

50g cashew nuts (optional)
75g baby corn, halved
4 button mushrooms, sliced
75g mangetout, halved
50g beansprouts
200g noodles (if you want to make this really quick and easy then use 'straight to the wok' noodles as they are pre-cooked)

1. First start by combining all the sauce ingredients in a small jug, mixing well.

2. If you are using dried noodles then cook them now by following the cooking instructions on the packet.

3. Heat the olive oil in a wok and add the carrot, shredded cabbage, cashew nuts and baby corn, cooking for 2 minutes.

4. Add the mushrooms, mangetout and stir, cooking for a further 2 minutes.

5. Add the beansprouts, noodles and the sauce, stir again and cook for a further 2 minutes.

Stuffed Pepper Bowls

A great recipe kids will love, and it doesn't matter if they don't eat all the pepper because they will love the rice and vegetables inside. It's packed with fibre and vitamins A, C and E. **Serves 2**

1 sweet red pepper per person, halved
75g uncooked long grain rice
300ml water
1 small onion, finely chopped
4 mushrooms, rinsed and chopped

4 runner beans, very finely sliced
30g Cheddar cheese, grated (optional)
Freshly ground black pepper
1 tsp dried or chopped fresh parsley

1. Cut peppers lengthwise into halves and remove seeds.

2. Bring a large saucepan of water to the boil. Place the peppers in and cook for about 5 minutes, until 'bendy' and drain.

While they are cooking prepare the filling.

3. Put the rice into a medium sized saucepan and pour on the water. Bring to the boil and then cover and simmer for about 10-15 minutes, until the rice is soft. If there is excess water drain it off before using the rice.

4. Put the olive oil in a shallow pan, cook the onion, mushrooms and runner beans for 5-7 minutes until soft, stirring regularly.

5. Stir in the cooked rice; season with ground black pepper and parsley.

6. Fill the pepper halves with the rice mixture and serve – nice with some grated cheese on top, it can either be eaten like this or put under a grill for a few minutes until the cheese has melted.

Tempting Taco Shells

This dish is and always has been a favourite with my two children. Let your children put them together themselves at the table; it makes it a much more fun meal and they like the feeling of independence. **Serves 2**

1 small onion, peeled and chopped
1 garlic clove, crushed
1 tbsp olive oil
1/2 red pepper, diced
1/2 small courgette, diced
400g tinned red kidney beans
400g tinned chopped tomatoes
2 closed cup mushrooms, diced

25g sweet corn
1/2 tsp dried mixed herbs

to serve
25g lettuce, washed and shredded
25g Cheddar cheese, finely grated
4 tbsp full fat natural yoghurt
Taco shells (2 per person)

1. Fry the onion and garlic in the oil, for 4-5 minutes, until softened, it will continue to cook as further ingredients are added .

2. Add the red pepper and courgette, and cook over a medium heat for a further 2-3 minutes.

3. Add the remaining ingredients and simmer over a low heat for a further 15 minutes, stirring regularly. While this is cooking pre-heat the oven to 180°C, gas 4.

4. Remove from the heat, cover and put aside.

5. Put the taco shells onto a baking tray and put in the warm oven for 2-3 minutes. Remove from the oven and allow to cool – they will crisp up as they cool.

6. To serve put 2 tbsp bean mixture in the taco shells, garnish with lettuce, finely grated cheese and a spoon of yoghurt on top.

Caitilin's Tip: You can make a large quantity of bean stew to freeze for another day. Try adding some chilli powder or dried chilli flakes according to your taste when you are frying the onion, to make a spicier meal.

Vegetable Kebabs

A great recipe for getting your children to help with; count the vegetables as you put them on the sticks, and talk about the different colours with them. You can choose any vegetables you like but I have selected the following tasty, colourful combination. **Serves 2**

2 kebab sticks (or the number of kebabs you require)

6 cherry tomatoes
1 courgette, washed and sliced 8mm thick

1 medium red onion, quartered
6 small button mushrooms
2 tbsp olive oil, to drizzle
1 tbsp dried mixed herbs
Freshly ground black pepper

1. Pre-heat the oven to 190°C, gas 5.

2. To make these kebabs simply divide the vegetables into equal portions (or the number of kebabs you are making) and slide the vegetables onto the kebab sticks in a fun and colourful pattern.

3. Line them up in an ovenproof dish and drizzle with the olive oil, sprinkle on the herbs and grind the pepper over them.

4. Place them in a moderate oven for 15-20 minutes, or until the vegetables are soft and slightly browned. Remove and serve.

Caitilin's Tip: I like cooking these outside in the summer on a BBQ. Make sure you watch your children if they help you make these as kebab sticks can be sharp – alternatively use popsicle sticks with rounded ends.

Watercress Ribbons with Cottage Cheese

Watercress is rich in iron, vitamin C, zinc, and folic acid and cottage cheese is full of calcium and vitamin D making a great combination with the delicate texture of tagliatelle. **Serves 1**

75g tagliatelle

1 tbsp olive oil
1 small onion, finely chopped

1 garlic clove, crushed
30g watercress, washed and chopped
50g cottage cheese
1 tbsp fresh parsley, finely chopped

1. Add the pasta to a large pan of boiling water, stir and return to the boil, cook for 7-9 minutes, until soft.
2. In a separate medium sized pan heat the olive oil and on a low heat gently fry the onion and garlic for 5-6 minutes, until soft. Add the watercress and stir, only cooking for 2 minutes.
3. Remove from the heat and stir in the cottage cheese and parsley, put aside.
4. Drain the pasta, mix in the watercress and cheese and serve.

Rocky Mountain Toast

All credit to my mum for this simple recipe, she came up with it when she was holidaying in the Rocky Mountains, USA and taught us when we were young. It has since become a firm favourite with my family and friends alike. Even though it is fried, only a very small amount of butter is used – only the amount you would put on a slice of bread, so it is still a healthy meal. **Serves 1**

1 slice wholemeal or brown bread
1 medium egg

3 cherry tomatoes, washed and sliced
Small knob of unsalted butter, for frying

1. Melt the butter in a frying pan.

2. Cut a small hole in the middle of the slice of bread about 2cm x 2cm square.

3. Put the bread in the frying pan and cook for approximately 2 minutes, until the bread is slightly browned. Using a spatula, turn the bread over and then crack the egg onto the bread so that the yolk is in the hole.

4. Put the tomatoes into the pan and allow them to cook, turning regularly.

5. Continue to cook for 2-3 minutes and turn the slice of bread with the egg over, cook for a further minute, allow to cool slightly and serve with the cooked tomatoes on top.

Mediterranean Couscous

Couscous provides plenty of taste and nourishment for a perfect meal in itself. Combined with a variety of bright and tasty vegetables this meal is also packed with essential vitamins. **Serves 2**

1 tbsp olive oil
1 small onion, chopped
1 garlic clove, crushed
4 small mushrooms, diced
1/2 sweet red or orange pepper, diced
1 small courgette, diced

8 cherry tomatoes, quartered
100g couscous
300ml vegetable stock
1 tsp fresh oregano, finely chopped
1 tsp fresh basil, finely chopped

1. Heat the olive oil in a medium sized saucepan and gently cook the onion, garlic, mushrooms, pepper, courgette and cherry tomatoes for 5-7 minutes until the vegetables are soft.

2. Add the dry couscous, stir and pour on the vegetable stock.

3. Add the oregano and basil and stir.

4. Cover with a lid and remove from the heat. Leave for 10 minutes until the couscous has absorbed all the liquid and is soft.

5. Fluff with a fork and if necessary re-heat gently, until hot through.

Basic Quiche

Quiches are simple to make and can be eaten hot or cold. You can add any vegetables such as courgettes, finely chopped broccoli, asparagus or olives. Packed with protein, and vitamins, they work really well with a baked potato and salad for a nutritious lunch or a light supper. **Serves 4**

250g short crust pastry
1 tbsp olive oil
1 red onion, chopped
2 large tomatoes, sliced
50g cheddar cheese, grated

125ml milk
1 free range egg
1 tsp fresh parsley, chopped
freshly ground pepper, to season

1. Pre-heat the oven to 190°C, gas 5.

2. Roll out the pastry to line a 22cm flan case (or shallow baking dish). Pierce the base and sides with a fork, this will allow the air to escape so the pastry will keep its shape on the tin. Put in the pre-heated oven for 10 minutes. Then take out and set to one side.

3. Heat the oil in a pan and gently fry the onion for 3-5 minutes, or until soft. Remove from the heat and allow to cool.

4. Spread the onion over the pastry base then cover with the sliced tomatoes.

5. Sprinkle on the grated cheese.

6. Pour the milk into a bowl and crack the egg into it, whisk until the egg and milk are combined. Add the parsley and the ground black pepper and whisk again. Pour this mixture over the pastry and vegetables.

7. Put in the pre-heated oven and bake for 30 minutes until browned and set.

Short Crust Pastry

100g plain flour, sifted
50g butter

3 tbsp cold water

1. Sift the flour in a medium sized mixing bowl and rub in the butter, until the mixture resembles breadcrumbs.

2. Pour the water into the mixture and stir with a fork. When the mixture sticks together it is ready to use. Do not overwork the pastry or get it too warm as it will become tough. Store in the fridge until using.

Simple Tomato Flan

I came across this recipe while we were in France one summer and the whole family loved it. When considering a healthy meal you may not think of a pastry dish but providing you don't eat pastry every day there is nothing wrong with it. This one works really well for lunch or dinner, either hot or cold with a juicy Greek salad. **Serves 2**

200g fresh ready rolled puff pastry
1/2 tsp fresh thyme, chopped
40g Cheddar cheese, grated
10 ripe cherry tomatoes, washed and
    sliced

2 tbsp fresh basil leaves, torn
1 tbsp olive oil

1. Pre-heat the oven to 200°C, gas 6.

2. Line a shallow baking dish with the puff pastry. Using a sharp knife, carefully score a line in the pastry, 1cm from the edges all the way round, but be careful not to cut it all the way through.

3. In a small bowl mix together the thyme and Cheddar cheese. Cover the pastry up to the scored line with this mixture.

4. Arrange the tomatoes in overlapping lines over the cheese and scatter on the basil leaves. Drizzle the olive oil over the top.

5. Bake in the pre-heated oven for 25 minutes. Remove and eat hot or allow to cool and take it on a picnic, or put it in a packed lunch box.

Cheesy Broccoli and Potato Bake

Broccoli is really one of those 'super vegetables', packed with iron, calcium and vitamins A and C. This dish has a lovely soft texture that children will love. If they aren't that keen on broccoli, suggest that they search for the hidden trees (broccoli) and eat them up like giants. **Serves 4**

200g broccoli, washed and roughly cut
1 small leek, washed and sliced (optional)
40g button mushrooms, washed and sliced
   (optional)

For the cheese sauce
300ml milk
3 level tbsp plain flour
Small knob unsalted butter

25g Cheddar cheese, grated
1 tbsp parsley, finely chopped

For the potato topping
3 medium sized potatoes, peeled and
   diced
4 tbsp full cream milk
Small knob unsalted butter

1. Pre-heat the oven to 190°C, gas 5.

2. Put the potatoes in a medium sized saucepan and cover with boiling water, return to the boil, turn down the heat, cover and cook for approximately 20 minutes, until soft.

If you have a steamer it is a really good idea to steam the broccoli and leeks over the potatoes while they are cooking. If not simply steam them in a small amount of water for 5-10 minutes, until soft. If using mushrooms cook for 5-7 minutes in a little butter.

3. To make the sauce put the milk, flour and butter into a saucepan, over a medium heat. Stir continuously (I tend to use a whisk thus ensuring it doesn't get lumpy) for about 5-10 minutes until the mixture thickens.

4. Add the grated cheese and parsley, and stir. The cheese will slightly thicken the sauce.

5. Put the vegetables into the sauce, stir and pour into a medium sized ovenproof dish and put aside.

6. Remove the potatoes from the heat, drain off the water and put them back into the saucepan. Add the butter and 4 tbsp milk to the potatoes and mash until soft and fluffy.

7. Put this on top of the vegetables and spread out evenly. Bake in the oven for 20 minutes, or until the top is slightly browned.

Flat Bread Pizzas

A healthy and simple way to make your own pizzas, and a favourite with all children. This recipe uses a simple tomato topping but you can use any topping you wish. **Serves 2**

Flat bread pizza base (use chapatti recipe on page 68 but add 1 tsp of olive oil to the mixture when the water is added)

For the topping
1 small onion, finely chopped
1 clove garlic, crushed
1 tbsp olive oil
200g tinned chopped tomatoes
Pinch dried mixed herbs

1. Pre-heat the oven to 200°C, gas 6.

2. In a small saucepan gently fry the onion and garlic in the olive oil for 3-4 minutes until soft. Add the chopped tomatoes and mixed herbs and cook gently for 10-15 minutes, stirring regularly.

While the sauce is cooking make the pizza bases.

3. When the sauce has cooked gently purée until any big pieces are gone.

4. Put the pizza bases onto dry pizza trays (if you do not have these then an ordinary baking tray is suitable).

5. Put 3 tbsp sauce onto each pizza base and cover evenly to within 1cm of the edge.

6. You can now just add some grated cheese or any other topping you prefer, such as sweet corn, sliced mushrooms, onion.

7. Put the pizzas in the pre-heated oven and bake for approximately 7 minutes or until the cheese has melted and slightly browned.

8. Remove from the oven, allow to cool slightly before serving as they are very hot when first taken out of the oven.

Lentil Pies

This healthy and nutritious meal, high in protein, iron and vitamin C, is still a favourite with us. This is quite a substantial recipe and makes a large enough quantity so the whole family can enjoy it together. Serves 4

Short crust pastry (page 58)

Pie filling
175g dried green lentils
2 button mushrooms, chopped
1 small onion, peeled and diced
1 garlic clove, crushed
1 tbsp olive oil
1 medium carrot, peeled and diced

1 stick celery, chopped
50g sweet corn
200g tinned chopped tomatoes
Pinch marjoram
100ml milk
1 free range egg
20g cottage cheese
Cheddar cheese (optional), **grated**

1. Firstly make the pastry and put aside in the fridge while you make the filling.

2. Cut the pastry in half, put half back in the fridge. Roll half on a floured surface to a 3mm thickness, put in a pie dish and bake it blind for 10 minutes by lining the pastry case with some greaseproof paper, pour in some ceramic baking beans or just use some dried beans or rice.

3. Rinse the lentils and cover with cold water. Cover the pan and bring to the boil. Boil rapidly for 10 minutes, reduce the heat and simmer for a further 20 minutes or until tender. While they are cooking prepare the remaining ingredients.

4. Fry the mushrooms, onion and garlic in the oil for 3 minutes and then add the carrot and celery, cook on a moderate heat for a further 5 minutes, stirring regularly, until the carrot is slightly softer.

5. Add the sweet corn, chopped tomatoes and marjoram.

6. Cover and cook on a low heat for a further 10 minutes, stirring regularly.

7. When the lentils are soft add them to the cooked vegetables, stir and cook for a further 10 minutes, stirring regularly.

8. Remove from the heat and put on top of the baked pastry. Put aside.

9. In a small mixing bowl combine the milk, egg and cottage cheese.

10. Pour this mixture onto the lentils.

11. Finally cover with the grated cheese. Roll the rest of the pastry out and place on top, sealing the edges with a fork. Ensure you now pierce the top to allow any trapped air to escape.

12. Bake in the pre-heated oven for 20-30 minutes, until the pastry is slightly browned.

Caitilin's Tip: I have used green lentils, but any variety will do.

Beany Couscous

My children love this quick and nutritious meal, packed with protein, iron, vitamin A and B. It works really well with some steamed green beans or spinach and some plain natural yoghurt. Serves 4

1 tbsp olive oil
1 small onion, chopped
1 garlic clove, crushed
100g tinned kidney beans
100g tinned chickpeas

200g couscous
200ml boiling vegetable stock
1 tsp fresh parsley, chopped
1 tsp fresh basil, chopped

1. Heat the olive oil in a medium sized saucepan and gently cook the onion and garlic for 4 minutes before adding the kidney beans, chickpeas and herbs. Mix together and cook gently for a further 5 minutes until the onion has softened and the beans are hot through.

2. Add the dry couscous, stir and pour on the boiling vegetable stock.

3. Turn off the heat and cover, leaving for 10 minutes until the couscous has absorbed all the water.

4. Fluff with a fork, sprinkle with chopped herbs and serve.

Spinach Pancake Rolls

An iron-rich meal that not only tastes good but looks good too. It may initially appear fiddly, but it is an easy meal which all the family can enjoy together.
Serves 3

100g fresh spinach, chopped
50g plain cottage cheese
40g Cheddar cheese, grated

For the sauce
2 tbsp olive oil
1 small onion, finely chopped
1 garlic clove, crushed

400g tin chopped plum tomatoes
Pinch dried mixed herbs

For the pancakes (makes 8)
100ml whole/semi-skimmed milk
1 medium egg, beaten
50g plain flour, sieved
20g butter

Pre-heat the oven to 220°C, gas 7.

Make the sauce first so it can cook while you are making the pancakes.

1. Gently fry the chopped onion and crushed garlic in the olive oil for 5 minutes, until softened, taking care not to burn the garlic or it will become very bitter.

2. Add the chopped tomatoes and mixed herbs and simmer gently for approximately 10 minutes, stirring frequently.

3. Remove the tomato sauce from the heat and purée until all the large pieces have gone. Put aside.

While this is cooking make the pancakes.

4. Pour the milk into a small mixing bowl, add the egg and whisk.

5. Add the flour and whisk until all the ingredients are combined and any lumps have been removed.

6. Put a small amount of butter in a non-stick frying pan and allow to melt. Add 3 tbsp of the pancake mixture to the frying pan. With the back of a spoon smooth it out to 3mm thickness and allow this side to cook. Flip the pancake over and cook the other side. Put aside and make the rest of the pancakes the same way. It is not necessary to keep them warm as they will be baked at the end of the recipe.

7. In a medium sized saucepan, steam the spinach in a little water until soft. Remove from the heat, drain and squeeze out any excess water and roughly chop.

8. Take 2 tbsp of the cooked spinach and put down the centre of one of the pancakes, put 1 tbsp cottage cheese on top of this and roll up the pancake. Place in a medium sized baking dish. Repeat this process for the remaining pancakes laying them in the dish side-by-side.

9. Pour the tomato sauce over the top of the pancakes. Finally sprinkle the grated cheese on top and bake in the pre-heated oven for 15-20 minutes, until the cheese has melted and slightly browned.

10. Remove from the oven and serve.

Caitilin's Tip: This dish works well with a simple salad.

Pancakes are not only great fun and quick to make but my children have always loved helping me weigh the ingredients, and mixing the batter. The toppings for them are endless – so experiment with whatever you like. Our favourite however has always simply been a little honey and some freshly squeezed lemon juice.

Eggy Veg

This is a delicious quick meal in one. Serves 1

Small knob butter
1 small cooked potato, finely diced
1 shallot, finely chopped
2 button mushrooms, finely chopped

1 egg, beaten
4 tbsp whole milk
1 tsp fresh herbs, finely chopped
2 tbsp Cheddar cheese, grated (optional)

1. Put the butter in the pan, add the cooked potato, shallot and mushrooms, stir and cook for 5-10 minutes, until soft.

2. Crack the egg into a small mixing bowl and beat together with the milk, and herbs.

3. Pour the egg mixture onto the vegetables and mix well. Cook for approximately 5 minutes, until the egg is set and cooked through.

4. Remove from the pan and sprinkle with a little cheese before serving.

Breads and Sweet Treats

Bread, in one form or another, has been one of the principal forms of food for humans from the earliest times. That hasn't really changed and today children love it as much as they always did.

Bread consists basically of flour and water and usually a yeast is used. Salt is present in most cases, but it is not necessary to include it in these breads for your children. The great thing about bread is it can be eaten with a huge variety of meals and you can experiment by adding a number of other ingredients such as spices (e.g. cinnamon), fruit (e.g. raisins), vegetables (e.g. onion), and nuts or seeds (e.g. poppy seeds).

The following recipes are just a few of my family's favourites, but feel free to experiment with your own ideas. I haven't included a recipe for pita bread but don't forget it as it's perfect for stuffing for a lunch or sliced into finger shapes for dipping.

People often assume that to be healthy you cannot have any sugar or chocolate in your diet, but that is far from the truth. As long as you give your children a healthy balanced diet packed with essential carbohydrates, protein, vitamins and nutrients then there is absolutely no reason why they can't have sweet cakes and biscuits occasionally. Just remember to try not to let sweets and sugary food be a quick fix to pacify your child when they are upset and don't always offer sweets as a reward. What I would say is anything in moderation is fine.

Chapattis

An easy alternative to bread. My children love these flatbreads and they are perfect for eating with cheese and cucumber or simply with a little butter. Alternatively use them as a pizza base (page 61). **Makes 3**

125g plain flour   **75ml cold water**

1. Sift the flour into a mixing bowl. Make a small well in the centre and pour in the water. Mix together to form a dough.

2. Knead the dough for 2-3 minutes on a lightly floured surface.

3. Divide into 3 equal sized pieces and roll each one to a 3mm thickness.

4. Heat a dry frying pan and put a chapatti in, cook for approximately 2 minutes, until browned. Turn the chapatti over and cook the other side, again until lightly browned.

Cheese Straws

A yummy snack, just right for in-between-meal times and they can be taken anywhere and are perfect for tiny hands. **Makes 10**

80g plain flour
40g butter, diced

5 tbsp cold water
20g Cheddar cheese

1. Pre-heat the oven to 180°C, gas 4.

2. Sift the flour into a mixing bowl and rub together with the butter until you have a breadcrumb texture.

3. Add the water and stir with a cold fork. Form into a ball.

4. Roll out the dough on a lightly floured surface to a 10mm thickness, sprinkle on the grated cheese. Roll the cheese into the pastry, fold the pastry in half and roll out again. Fold in half a second time and roll the pastry to a 5mm thickness.

5. With either a knife or a pastry cutter cut into 2 x 6cm rectangles.

6. Place on a baking tray and bake in the centre of the oven for 15 minutes, until slightly browned. Remove and cool before serving.

Caitilin's Tip: It is quite useful to make these cheese straws when you have made a pie and have some left over pastry. Cheese straws are perfect to use with dips (page 26).

Instead of just cutting them into rectangles try taking two sausages of pastry and twisting them together.

Fun Seeded Breads

For this recipe get your children to help choose the seeds and roll the bread in them once it is made. **Makes 6**

250g strong white flour
200g wholemeal bread flour
25g butter
7g quick acting dried yeast
300ml warm water
3 tbsp milk

To decorate
20g poppy seeds
20g sesame seeds
20g sunflower seeds

1. In a large mixing bowl combine the flours and rub in the butter, add the yeast, mix it in.

2. Make a well in the centre and pour in the warm water. Mix until the ingredients stick together to form a dough.

3. Put the dough onto a clean floured surface and knead well, for approximately 5-10 minutes, until the dough has an elastic texture.

4. Divide into small balls (5-10cm) or any shape of your choice.

5. Paint milk onto the top of each bun.

6. Put the seeds into 3 separate saucers and get your toddler to sprinkle them on the top of each bun, or roll the buns in the seeds.

7. Pre-heat the oven to 220°C, gas 7.

8. Lightly grease a baking tray and put the buns onto it, cover with a clean damp cloth, to stop them drying out. Leave to rise in a warm place for approximately 30 minutes or until the dough has doubled in size.

9. Put in the oven and bake for approximately 20 minutes, they will sound hollow when tapped on the base.

10. Remove from the oven and allow to cool on a rack before eating.

Garlic Bread

Garlic bread is a great accompaniment to soups and pasta dishes and my children love it as they use their fingers to eat it and yes they are supposed to.

There are two ways to make it, you can either spread the garlic butter on some homemade toast or on a sliced baguette. It's best to make your own bread as its fresh and you will know exactly what is in it. If you don't have the time to make your own don't worry it will taste just as good. **Serves 2**

4 slices brown bread or 1 small baguette
25g unsalted butter
1 garlic clove, crushed

Pinch mixed herbs
Freshly ground black pepper

1. In a small dish mash the butter with a fork until soft.

2. Add the garlic, herbs and black pepper and mash with the butter.

3. Spread the garlic butter onto sliced toast and grill for 1-2 minutes until the butter has browned. If you are using a baguette then partially slice it and spread the butter between the slices. Put it in a pre-heated oven (180°C/gas 5) for 10-12 minutes, until the garlic butter has melted and the bread is slightly crispy on the outside.

Onion Bread

My mum always used to make this for us to eat warm with some butter to dip in soups or as sandwiches. It is really easy to make and has a great flavour. Even if your children don't like onions, it's okay because you can chop them really finely and they won't even know they are there. **Makes 1 large loaf**

1 tbsp olive oil
1 small onion, finely chopped
450g strong white flour

25g butter
7g quick acting dried yeast
300ml warm water

1. Very gently sauté the onion in the olive oil for 5-7 minutes until soft, ensuring it doesn't go too brown. Remove from the heat and put aside.

2. In a large mixing bowl combine the flour and butter, add the yeast. Make a well in the centre and pour in the warm water. Mix until the ingredients come together to form a dough.

3. Put the dough onto a clean floured surface and knead well for approximately 10 minutes, until the dough has an elastic texture.

4. Flatten the dough out to 5cm thickness and add the onion, knead this in for 1-2 minutes until the onion is spread throughout the dough. Form into one large round loaf, the shape is not important as it has a rustic look when finished.

5. Pre-heat the oven to 220°C, gas 7.

6. Lightly grease a baking tray and put the bread onto it and leave to rise for approximately 45 minutes until the dough has doubled in size.

7. Put in the oven and bake for approximately 35 minutes. It will be cooked when you hear a hollow sound if you tap on the bottom of the bread.

8. Remove from the oven and cool slightly on a rack before slicing and eating.

Caitilin's Tip: Another tasty combination is olive and sun-dried tomato bread, just substitute the onion for the 40g chopped olives and 8 chopped sun-dried tomatoes – they do not need to be pre-cooked.

Sweet Cinnamon and Fruit Bread

This has always been a favourite after-school snack, again introduced to me by my mother – she always made the yummiest bread (and still does). My children love dried fruit so I add raisins and apricots to the recipe, which not only taste good but are also rich sources of fibre, potassium and iron. **Makes 1 large loaf**

500g strong white flour
25g butter
7g quick acting dried yeast
300ml warm water

30g raisins or currants
30g dried apricots, finely chopped
2 tsp ground cinnamon
5 tbsp runny honey

1. In a large mixing bowl combine the flour and butter and mix in the yeast. Make a well in the centre and pour in the warm water. Mix until the ingredients come together to form a dough.

2. Put the dough onto a clean floured surface and knead well for approximately 10 minutes, until the dough has an elastic texture.

3. Pre-heat the oven to 220°C, gas 7.

4. Slightly flatten the dough to 3cm thickness and spread the honey over the surface within 2cm of the edges. Sprinkle on the dried fruit and evenly sprinkle with ground cinnamon.

5. Roll up the dough and make into a long flattish loaf shape.

6. Lightly grease a baking tray and put the bread onto it. Leave it to rise in a warm place for approximately 45 minutes, or until the dough has doubled in size.

7. Put in the oven and bake for approximately 25-35 minutes, until risen and browned. When turned over and tapped a hollow sound can be heard.

8. Remove from the oven and cool on a cooling rack before slicing and eating – yummy served simply with a small amount or butter, also best if eaten when warm, mmmm.

Apple Cake Surprise

This moist cake is delicious eaten warm either as a treat or as a pudding, perhaps served with some homemade custard. **Serves 6**

125g cooking margarine
125g caster sugar
1/2 tsp vanilla essence
1/2 tsp cinnamon

1 medium egg
125g self raising flour, sifted
2 dessert apples, peeled and sliced

1. Pre-heat the oven to 190°C, gas 5.

2. Cream the cooking margarine and sugar until light and fluffy.

3. Add the vanilla essence, cinnamon and whole egg, beat together until all the ingredients are evenly combined. Add the flour and stir until combined and the mixture looks smooth.

4. Line a deep, 20cm cake tin with grease-proof paper, layer the sliced apples in the bottom of the tin and pour the cake mixture on top of them.

5. Put into the pre-heated oven (warning; hot oven, the adult must do this part) and bake for approximately 20-25 minutes until the cake has risen and slightly browned. The best way to test if the cake is done is to insert a clean knife into the middle of the cake and if it comes out clean it is done.

Autumn Crumble

A pudding for the whole family. Your little one will love the sweet, tangy flavour, combined with the rough textured topping. Serve with some homemade custard or natural yoghurt. **Serves 3**

1 ripe dessert apple, peeled, cored and chopped
2 fresh rhubarb stalks, chopped into 2cm pieces
20g blackberries, fresh or tinned
1 tbsp brown sugar or honey
1 tsp ground cinnamon
200ml water
1 tsp cornflour

For the crumble topping
60g plain flour
30g butter
20g brown sugar
10g rolled oats

1. Pre-heat the oven to 180°C, gas 4.

2. Put the prepared fruit in a medium sized saucepan with the sugar (or honey) and cinnamon, add the water and bring to the boil. Turn down and simmer for 10 minutes or until the fruit is soft.

3. While the fruit is simmering make the crumble topping. Put the flour and butter in a bowl and work together with your finger tips until it reaches a fine breadcrumb consistency. Add the sugar and oats and mix together.

4. Remove the fruit from the heat. To thicken the juice put the cornflour in a cup add 2 tablespoons of cold water and mix. Pour this onto the cooked fruits, return to the heat and stir for 2-3 minutes, until the juices have thickened.

5. Put the fruit into a medium (20cm) ovenproof dish and put the crumble topping on top.

6. Bake in the oven for 15-20 minutes, or until the top is slightly browned. Allow to cool slightly before serving.

Banana and Blueberry Muffins

Perfect for snacks and lunch boxes, muffins are a favourite not only with children but with mums and dads too. These are really easy to make and are very versatile as you can add any fruit you like. Blueberries are full of vitamins and antioxidants, and in fact one serving of blueberries contains as many valuable antioxidants as five servings of apples, carrots or broccoli. If your little one doesn't usually like blueberries then try this recipe as once they are cooked they have a much richer and sweeter flavour than if you just eat them raw. **Serves 8**

150g plain flour
1 tsp baking powder
1/2 tsp ground cinnamon
1 ripe banana, cut into chunks
1 egg

60g soft brown sugar
45g butter, softened
1/2 tsp vanilla extract
40g blueberries, washed

1. Preheat oven to 190°C, gas 5.

2. In a medium sized mixing bowl sift together the flour, baking powder and ground cinnamon. Put aside.

3. Purée the banana in a blender until all the lumps have gone.

4. Add the egg, brown sugar, softened butter and vanilla extract and blend again, until these ingredients are combined. Pour this mixture into the flour and stir well to combine. Gently fold through the blueberries.

5. Spoon the mixture into greased 7cm muffin tins (or in baking cases) and bake for 25 minutes until risen and golden brown.

6. Cool in the tin for 10 minutes, remove from the tin and put on a wire rack to finish cooling.

Caitilin's Tip: The muffins will keep for 3-4 days if sealed in an airtight container. Instead of blueberries you can use other berries such as blackberries or raspberries, they taste just as good, so use whatever you have available or combine all three.

Banana Cakes

This simple cake mixture is healthy and tasty at the same time. Little cakes are a perfect way to get your toddler involved in the cooking, they love to be part of it – especially mixing together the gooey ingredients. **Makes approximately 12 cakes**

125g cooking margarine
125g caster sugar
1/2 tsp vanilla essence
1/2 tsp cinnamon

1 ripe banana, roughly chopped
1 medium egg
125g self raising flour, sifted

1. Pre-heat the oven to 190°C, gas 5.

2. Cream together the cooking margarine and sugar until light and fluffy.

3. Add the vanilla essence, cinnamon, banana and whole egg, beat together until all ingredients are well mixed.

4. Put the self raising flour into the mixture and mix until all the ingredients are evenly combined.

5. This is where the help of your little one is really needed. Put 12 baking cases into a cupcake tray and spoon the mixture evenly between the 12 cases. Put into the pre-heated oven (warning; hot oven, the adult must do this part) and bake for 10-12 minutes until the cakes have risen and are slightly browned.

Caitilin's Tip: Test if the cakes are done by inserting a clean knife into the middle of one of the cakes and if it comes out clean it is done.

It doesn't matter how messy the cakes look before they go into the oven as I find that they always seem to come out perfect after they have been cooked.

You can also use this recipe to make chocolate banana cakes. Simply add 25g cocoa powder to the mixture when the flour is added.

Crispy Cakes

A quick and easy way to make a special chocolate treat. These are great for birthday parties and your little ones will love to help with the cooking. **Makes 5**

100g plain chocolate
30g unsalted butter

50g rice crispies or cornflakes
25g sultanas

1. Break the chocolate into small pieces and place in a medium sized mixing bowl. Put this bowl into a medium sized saucepan half-full of boiling water (an adult must do this part). Stir the chocolate allowing it to melt. Add the butter and melt this into the chocolate, stirring together. Try not to let any of the water get into the chocolate.

2. Put the rice crispies or cornflakes and sultanas in a second medium sized mixing bowl.

3. Pour the chocolate over them and mix.

4. Spoon into small baking cases and allow to cool and set before eating.

Frozen Surprise

Children love this nutritious treat as they can help pick out the fruit and make it with you every step of the way. It is perfect for a summer's day or at a birthday party. You can choose any combination of fruits for this delicious recipe. **Makes 1**

2 strawberries, finely chopped
2 tbsp tinned crushed pineapple

1/2 banana cut in small cubes
2 tbsp pure orange juice

1. Mix ingredients together and put into a plastic cup.

2. Put in the freezer and freeze.

3. Remove from the freezer and serve partially defrosted either in the cup, or turned out in a bowl, it will keep its shape and look fun too.

Gramma's Cookies

My mum always made the best cookies, every night without fail after supper we would have the yummiest freshest warm cookies. Any dried fruit can be used and a real treat is to add some chocolate chips. **Makes 8**

50g soft brown sugar
60g butter
1/2 tsp vanilla essence

75g plain flour
25g raisins

1. Pre-heat the oven to 180°C, gas 4.

2. Put the sugar and butter into a small mixing bowl and cream together until light and fluffy.

3. Add the vanilla essence and flour, mix and lastly add the raisins, mixing with your hands to form a smooth dough.

4. Take a small amount of dough and roll into a ball in the palms of your hands, place onto a greased baking tray and squash to 1cm thickness.

5. Place in the pre-heated oven (an adult must do this part) and bake for 10-12 minutes. Remove and allow to cool slightly on a wire rack before eating.

Caitilin's Tip: Try either 1/2 tsp grated washed orange or lemon rind instead of vanilla.

Chocolate Nests

A small amount of chocolate in a healthy diet is absolutely fine and these are a great way to make a special Easter treat. Every year I make them with my own children and also with the local children in my parent and toddler group. **Makes 4**

100g plain chocolate
75g Shredded wheat

Mini chocolate eggs or raspberries to
  decorate

1. Break the chocolate into small pieces and place in a medium sized mixing bowl. Put this bowl into a medium sized saucepan half-full of boiling water (an adult must do this part). Stir the chocolate allowing it to melt. Try not to let any of the water get into the chocolate.

2. In a second medium sized mixing bowl crush the Shredded wheat and add the melted chocolate to this. Mix and spoon into baking cases.

3. Decorate the nests with little chocolate eggs or raspberries and allow to cool, therefore allowing the chocolate to harden.

Fruit Bars

Dried fruit is a favourite with my children and when combined in these delicious bars it makes a healthy snack for your toddler at any time of day. Remember they are also great for lunch boxes. **Makes 12**

60g dried apricots
20g figs
10g raisins

10g dried apple
6 small sheets rice paper

1. Put all the fruit into a blender. Combine until the fruit is puréed and the mixture sticks together. Put to one side.

2. Place a piece of rice paper on a clean dry surface and spoon the fruit mixture onto it.

3. Put a second piece of rice paper on top and roll the 'sandwich' to a 5mm thickness. Then using a sharp knife cut into rectangles.

Caitilin's Tip: Keep the fruit bars in a sealed container in the fridge as it keeps them firm and fresh. They can last this way for up to a month.

Fruity Flapjacks

A great way to get your little ones involved is to allow them to help weigh the ingredients and stir the mixture when required. Fruity flapjacks are also a great way of adding vitamins to a sweet treat. Any dried fruits can be used. **Makes 8**

140g unsalted butter
40g rolled oats
6 apricots, finely chopped

8 dates, finely chopped
150g demerara sugar

1. Pre-heat the oven to 190°C, gas 5.

2. Melt the butter in a small saucepan (do not allow it to bubble).

3. Combine the oats, dried fruit and sugar in a large mixing bowl. Pour the butter onto this mixture and stir with a wooden spoon until the mixture sticks together.

4. Spread this mixture evenly onto a greased baking tray 2cm thick.

5. Bake in the oven for 15 minutes, until golden brown.

6. Remove from the oven and cool slightly. Cut into rectangles while still warm, but allow to cool in the tray before removing. As they cool the oats will stick together.

Healthy Carrot Cake

Carrot cake was always a favourite of mine, so this healthy recipe is a really easy way to make either one cake or a number of smaller cakes – perfect as a treat or at parties. Also a great recipe to get your children involved. **Makes 1 large cake or 9 small cakes**

175g self raising flour
2 tsp baking powder
125g muscovado sugar
1 tsp ground cinnamon
Pinch ground nutmeg
150ml sunflower oil
3 eggs, beaten

1 tsp vanilla extract
250g carrots, peeled and grated

Frosting (optional)
75g cream cheese
1 tsp vanilla extract
50g icing sugar

1. Pre-heat oven to 180°C, gas 4.

2. In a large mixing bowl sift together the flour and baking powder, add the sugar, cinnamon and nutmeg, stir and then make a well in the centre.

3. Pour in the oil, eggs, vanilla extract and grated carrots.

4. Pour the mixture into a lined, 20cm cake tin or if you are making smaller cakes then line a tray with bun cases and spoon the mixture in.

5. Bake in the pre-heated oven for 25-30 minutes (buns) until well risen and golden brown. If you are making one cake then increase the baking time by 10 minutes. Cool on a wire rack.

6. To make the frosting simply mix all the ingredients together until smooth. When the cake has cooled swirl on top using a teaspoon.

Scones

These are brilliant snacks for the whole family, which can be kept for up to a week in a sealed container. They can be enjoyed with any topping, but being brought up and living in Cornwall we love them with jam and clotted cream – but it's only once in a while. **Makes 8**

200g plain flour
3 tsp baking powder
25g butter

25g caster sugar
150ml milk

1. Pre-heat the oven to 200°C, gas 6.

2. In a medium sized mixing bowl sift the flour and baking powder together.

3. Rub in the butter, until it forms a breadcrumb-like texture.

4. Add the sugar and mix together.

5. Make a well in the centre and pour in the milk. Using your hands make into a soft dough.

6. Take the dough out of the bowl and knead quickly for 1-2 minutes on a floured surface.

7. Roll the dough out to 1-1.5 cm thick and using cutters cut out the scones.

8. Place them on a lightly greased baking tray and brush the tops with milk.

9. Bake in the oven for 10-12 minutes. When lightly browned remove from the oven and allow to cool slightly on a wire rack before serving.

Caitilin's Tip: Add 20g raisins to the dough to make fruity scones.

Fun Fruity Kebabs

Fruits are a vital (and easy) component to all healthy diets and children of all ages love them. Kiwi fruits contain almost twice as much vitamin C as oranges. In fact one kiwi fruit supplies more than the daily adult requirement of vitamin C. The dark colour of the flesh means it is packed full of goodness. Pink grapefruit contains a powerful antioxidant lycopene (more commonly found in tomatoes, but also present here and in watermelon) which is not present in an ordinary grapefruit, so it's a great idea to introduce more unusual and different fruits to your little ones.

A very simple alternative to an ordinary fruit salad, it's great fun to make and your children can help choose the fruits and put the kebabs together with you. It's also a really good way to talk about colours and patterns in a fun and tasty way.

You can choose any fruits you like but I have chosen the following combination.

2 popsicle sticks (or the number of kebabs you require)
6 strawberries
6 cubes of fresh melon
2 kiwi fruits, peeled and cubed
6 green grapes
6 purple grapes

To make these kebabs simply divide the fruit into two equal amounts (or the number of kebabs you are making) and slide the fruit onto the popsicle sticks in a fun and colourful pattern.

These are tasty eaten on their own or dipped into natural plain yoghurt.

Smoothies and Milkshakes

Smoothies and milkshakes are a very easy and fun way to get fruit and other nutritious foods into your child's diet. They can also be an excellent source of calcium – particularly for children who don't like milk. Young children also need the energy from the fat in full fat milk. Soya milks should be fortified with calcium, vitamin B12 and vitamin D if used as an alternative to cow's milk for young children.

My eldest daughter Skylar (now aged 5) is not keen to drink milk on its own, but as soon as it is made into a fruity milkshake, or smoothie she loves it. All you need is a blender and a few simple ingredients. Blend with fruit juice or add milk, yoghurt, or frozen yoghurt for a creamier drink.

You can use your choice of fresh fruit, frozen fruit such as berries, and even tinned pineapple or peaches (strain the syrup first). The list for these healthy drinks, for any time of the day is endless. The following recipes are just a few of my children's favourites. But feel free to experiment with any combination of fruits and berries you have to hand.

Basic Banana

Serves 2

1 small banana, cut in chunks
6 tbsp plain low-fat yoghurt
4 tbsp pure orange juice

1. Put all ingredients in blender and whirl until smooth. This will be fairly thick but simply add more liquid if required.

2. To make this into a milkshake instead of using yoghurt and orange juice simply add whole milk and blend to a frothy drink. If it's a hot day then 2 added ice cubes make it really refreshing.

Bubbly Berries

Serves 1

6 strawberries
6 raspberries
6 blackberries

3 tbsp plain natural yoghurt, or
for more of a milkshake use 40ml whole organic milk

1. Put the berries in a blender and purée until smooth.

2. Add the milk or yoghurt (or both) and blend again until the ingredients are mixed.

3. Serve cold.

Clever Crumble Smoothie

Almost like a pudding or a breakfast on its own. Serves 2

5 blackberries
5 raspberries
1 tbsp fine cut porridge oats
1 tbsp natural live yoghurt

1/2 apple, peeled and diced or 75ml pure apple juice
1 teaspoon honey (optional)

Put all the ingredients in a blender and blend until smooth. Enjoy.

Cool Kiwi

Serves 2

1 kiwi fruit, peeled and diced
1/2 mango, peeled and diced

1 tbsp plain natural yoghurt
1 tsp runny honey (optional)

Put all the ingredients in a blender and blend until smooth. Enjoy.

Fruity and Fresh

Serves 1

1/2 mango, peeled and diced
1 ripe nectarine, peeled, de-stoned and diced
Squeeze of fresh lemon

Put all the ingredients in a blender and whiz until smooth.

Soft Summery Smoothie

Serves 2

Peach, peeled and de-stoned
Seedless green grapes

¼ melon, peeled and seeds removed
50ml pure apple juice

Put all the ingredients in a blender and blend until smooth.

Super Standard Smoothie

Serves 2

1 orange, chopped
1 ripe banana, chopped

1 ripe apple, peeled, cored and diced
2-3 tbsp orange juice

Put in a blender and purée until smooth. Add more orange juice if required.

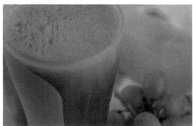

Weekly Meal Plans

When feeding a toddler it can be very daunting knowing where to start and it can help to begin with the idea that toddlers need a lot less to eat than you think, approximately 1/4 serving size of an adult. As toddlers have little tummies and use a lot of energy it is really important that they eat little and often so snacks for growing toddlers are essential. It is important to have a variety of fresh foods as opposed to large quantities of one particular thing. The following suggested meal plans will take you over a 3 week period with breakfast, lunch, dinner and healthy snacks for those hungry in-between-times.

When it comes to snacks I often find that a simple mixture of dried and fresh fruit is easy and always to hand with no cooking necessary. Add this into your day when ever you/they like. Another tip is with each meal to give them some diluted pure fruit juice or water or milk to drink. I prefer and always use these healthy drinks as opposed to commercial fruit squash drinks etc, which are full of unnecessary sugars, additives and preservatives.

I have taken this healthy plan roughly from meals we as a family eat at home together. Each week contains the required amounts of carbohydrates, proteins, fibre, calcium and vitamins. Use it as a guide and add your own meals from the book as you get used to the idea. It can also be used not only for your children but for the whole family to enjoy together. So get cooking.

Week One

	Monday	Tuesday	Wednesday
Breakfast	One weetabix with chopped banana and whole milk Pure orange juice	Shreddies with whole milk Pure orange juice	Boiled egg with toasted soldiers to dip One satsuma Milk to drink
Lunch	Hummus with crunchy vegetable dippers Small brown bread cheddar cheese sandwich	Jacket potato boats with cucumber and cherry tomatoes Fruity yoghurt	Pasta with rainbow sauce and grated cheese on top 1 piece of fruit
Dinner	Tasty lentil bolognese Greek salad	Rocky mountain toast with tomatoes Rice pudding	Asparagus risotto with crunchy green salad and natural plain yoghurt
Snack Ideas	Pancakes Dried fruit bars	Frozen surprise Oatcakes	Healthy carrot cake

Thursday	Friday	Saturday	Sunday
Porridge with honey to sweeten and whole milk Chopped apple Pure orange juice	Cereal with added fresh strawberries Pure apple juice	Mixed fruit salad of banana, kiwi, orange and blueberries Toast and honey Milk to drink	Scrambled egg on toast Pure orange juice
Chapatti with Cheddar cheese, cucumber, and sliced avocado Fruity flapjacks	Brown bread egg and cress sandwiches Fruit kebabs	Tasty lentil soup with toast or garlic bread Mini fruit salad	Pita bread with cottage cheese, cucumber and grated carrot Banana cake
Creamy beetroot in a potato boat	Chunky bean soup with garlic bread	Roast vegetable lasagne and Greek salad	Chickpea and aubergine stew Crispy sweet vegetable medly
Fruit salad	Apricot fruit bars	Rice cakes and fruit	Fruity yoghurt

Week Two

	Monday	Tuesday	Wednesday
Breakfast	Toast Fruity yoghurt Pure fruit juice	Cereal Piece of fruit Pure fruit juice	Boiled egg and soldiers Pure fruit juice
Lunch	Watercress soup & croutons Fruity flapjack	Raw vegetables and dips Banana and blueberry muffin	Pasta and pesto Fun fruity kebabs
Dinner	Roasted squashy rice with stripy rainbow salad	Tempting taco shells	Baby vegetables and tofu with rice noodles Healthy carrot cake
Snack Ideas	Basic banana smoothie and cheese straws	Pancakes	Smoothie Apple cake surprise

Thursday	Friday	Saturday	Sunday
Weetabix and strawberries Pure fruit juice	Toast Fun fruity kebab	Cereal Toast Pure fruit juice	Scrambled egg Pure fruit juice
Simple cheese and cucumber sandwich Fruity yoghurt	Baked potato boats Tomato and feta cheese salad	Hearty lentil soup and mini bread to dip	Pita bread sandwich Piece of fresh fruit
Beany couscous Fresh vegetables	Watercress ribbons with cottage cheese Gramma's cookies	Cheesy potato and broccoli bake Garlic bread	Beany couscous Greek salad
Fruit bar	Rice cakes Milkshake	Frozen surprise	Bowl of chopped fresh fruit and dried fruit

Week Three

	Monday	Tuesday	Wednesday
Breakfast	Boiled egg with soldiers Pure fruit juice	Berry milkshake Toast	Weetabix with yoghurt and banana
Lunch	Tomato soup with croutons Piece of fresh fruit	Cottage cheese and tomato sandwich on brown bread Fresh and dried fruit mixture	Baked sweet potatoes Fresh fruit
Dinner	Ratatouille Creamy spinach mash	Mild creamy curry Rice and plain natural yoghurt	Roast vegetable lasagne Crunchy green salad
Snack Ideas	Fruity flapjacks Small bunch grapes	Sweet cinnamon and fruit bread	Dried fruit Milkshake

Thursday	Friday	Saturday	Sunday
Cereal with whole milk Pure fruit juice	Toast Smoothie	Rocky mountain toast Pure fruit juice	Cereal with whole milk Pure fruit juice
Toasted cheese, tomato, red sweet pepper and sweetcorn sandwich Fun fruity kebab	Cool arrabiata Fresh fruit	Hummus dip with raw vegetables and pita bread fingers	Creamy mushroom soup Small bowl of blueberries chopped orange and sliced apple
Chickpea and aubergine stew Salad of your choice	Creamy leek and potato soup Garlic bread and cheese fingers to dip	Cheesy broccoli and potato bake Simple green salad	Lentil pies Couscous salad Yoghurt
Cheese straws Fresh fruit	Dried fruit bars	Frozen surprise	Pancakes and fresh fruit

Index